Breifne

FROM CHIEFTAIN TO LANDLORD

Breifne

FROM CHIEFTAIN TO LANDLORD

Mary Weir

N

First published 2009

Nonsuch Publishing
119 Lower Baggot Street
Dublin 2
Ireland
www.nonsuchireland.com

British Library Cataloguing in Publication Data.
A catalogue record for this book is available from the British Library.

ISBN 978 1 8458 8963 0

Typesetting and origination by The History Press
Printed in Great Britain

PAGE 61 - 66

Contents

1   The Story of Dervorgilla, Tighernan and Dermot   7

2   The Story of Brian O'Rourke (Brian of the Ramparts) 1564-1591   30

3   Brian Oge O'Rourke (Brian of the Battleaxes) 1584-1604   51

4   The Villiers Connection   71

5   Plantation and the Rising of 1641   94

6   The Age of the Landlord: 1800-1906   115

7   List of Sources   158

The Story of Dervorgilla, Tighernan and Dermot

Sometime in the year 1152, Tighernan O'Rourke, King of Breifne, went on a pilgrimage to Lough Derg. There, he prayed and ruminated over the disastrous state of his affairs. The people of Conmaicne had revolted against him and had succeeded in breaking free from his control. His former ally, Turlough O'Connor, whom he had supported in his bid for the High Kingship, had deserted him and burned his stronghold near the Shannon. O'Connor had even been involved in a plot to kill him. O'Rourke saw the doom of his dream to expand his kingdom into North Connaught. In his despair he must have felt that matters could not have been worse. But he was wrong. Whilst he prayed at Lough Derg, a dramatic event was unfolding back at his castle in Breifne – his wife Dervorgilla eloped with his enemy Dermot MacMurrough, King of Leinster.

Many claims were later made about this extraordinary event – that it was an abduction not an elopement and even more remarkably, that it caused the Norman Invasion in 1169. The only two contemporary accounts referring to the event are, firstly, the report of the Norman Invasion called *Expugnatio Hibernica* by the Welshman Giraldus Cambrensis and secondly, the epic poem *The Song of Dermot and the Earl* whose author is unknown. There are also *The Annals of the Four Masters* written some hundreds of years later but transcribed from earlier texts. All of these regard the event as an elopement. Henry II would find reasons for advancing into Ireland but the enmity of Dermot MacMurrough and Tighernan O'Rourke was of importance in the lead-up to the Norman Invasion.

Tighernan O'Rourke was descended from the ancient dynasty of Uí Briúin which was based in Carnfree, Co. Roscommon around AD 700. Later, some of the group, the Uí Briúin Breifne, moved north-east and settled in an area which is now north Leitrim and north-west Cavan. It became known as Breifne. The chief family of the Uí Briúin Breifne was the Uí Ruairc family. The Uí Ruairc family was to rule Breifne for over 700 years. Indeed so powerful did they become between the tenth and twelfth centuries that Tighernan could number four kings of Connaught among his ancestors. By the twelfth century, Breifne had expanded southwards and eastwards to encompass the territory of present-day Leitrim, Cavan and Longford as well as northern parts of counties Sligo, Roscommon and Meath. It is described in the *Annals* as the Kingdom of Uí Briúin and Conmaicne.

The O'Rourkes lived as Gaelic chieftains extracting rents or tributes from their under-lords. The chief (Taoiseach) was chosen from the male line of the extended family on the basis of suitability; bravery, power and popularity. There was no distinction between legitimate and illegitimate sons, all having equal rights. In any case the successor (or Tánaiste) was not necessarily a son. This led to fierce internecine rivalry within families, manifesting itself in blindings or castrations to render a candidate unfit to be Taoiseach. Killings were common among fathers, sons, uncles and cousins. The fact that Brehon law allowed for four wives, coupled with the practice of fostering out children, made for loose family ties. As late as the sixteenth century Bryan O'Rourke is reputed to have had one and possibly two of his brothers slain, before he became Prince of Breifne.

It was this kind of struggle that led to the first meeting of Tighernan and Dervorgilla in 1122. She was fourteen years old and he, at thirty, was sixteen years her senior. In fact the circumstance of their meeting is a good example of how things were done in the twelfth century. The King of Breifne, Aedh Sronmael (the flat-nosed) O'Rourke, led an unsuccessful raid on the Kingdom of Meath and was killed by Murchadh Ua Maeleachlainn, King of Meath. Aedh was Tighernan's cousin but any thoughts of revenge were forgotten when Tighernan discovered that Murchadh now supported him as the next King of Breifne. In addition Murchadh offered his young daughter Dervorgilla in marriage to

Tighernan. Dervorgilla's mother was the well-born Mor, daughter of a high king. The *Annals* refer to Mor as 'most gracious Queen of Ireland'.

Tighernan was an up-and-coming, ambitious man. A warrior of formidable energies, he was keen from the start of his rule to extend his kingdom far beyond its original boundaries. Marriage to the highly eligible Dervorgilla would serve to raise his sights further in the direction of Meath.

When Dervorgilla made her journey from Meath to Breifne accompanied by her attendants, she brought with her a large dowry of cattle, horses and furniture. She probably approached Breifne along the ancient highway into north Leitrim through Ballintogher. It must have been strange and difficult for her, moving from the plains of Meath to an area full of mountains, steep valleys and lakes.

The Breifne Kingdom of O'Rourke was isolated, bleak and almost inaccessible except through the routes offered by the glens of Glencar, Glenade and Glenfarne. The mountains of Dartry, Arigna and Slieve Anieran formed impenetrable boundaries. The soil was marshy, boggy, waterlogged. But, of course, the landscape was dramatic; the vistas from the hills of Glencar and Slieve Anieran are of incomparable beauty. Giraldus describes Ireland as a land 'overgrown with vast and ever-multiplying woods'. This was certainly true of Breifne. The woods were full of boar, wild pigs and deer. Grouse, quail and wild peacocks abounded. Tracks led to clearings where small black cattle and sheep grazed. Wolves and foxes were numerous. Giraldus gives a lyrical description of the eagle 'looking straight at the very rays of the sun with all its brightness and so high does it soar in its flight that its wings are scorched by the burning fires of the sun'. Dervorgilla too may well have watched the eagles soaring in the hills of Glenade or Glencar as she approached.

The O'Rourkes had many strongholds but the principal seat was at Dromahaire, though there was an earlier seat at Woodford near Newtowngore. It is not certain where exactly Devorgilla resided as the O'Rourkes also had an island fortress in Garadice Lake close to Woodford.

As wife of the King of Breifne, Dervorgilla presided over a household engaged in the preparation of food and the spinning and weaving of wool for clothing. The Irish banquet had a lavish menu. As well as the beef and mutton from the herds, hunting of the wild boar ensured a plentiful supply of pork. Honey from the hives of wild bees was the source of mead, which was the common drink along with imported wine. At the banquet, a poem composed by the file (poet) was recited accompanied by the music of the harp. The themes were generally in praise of the king's noble lineage, his generosity as host or his bravery in battle. Sometimes they had a sharper edge spurring the King into war or mocking his enemies. The standard and quality of the music of the harp and the tinpanum (a brass instrument with strings played with a plectrum) was excellent, judging by the astonishment of Giraldus at the 'speed and skill of the fingers'. He declares, 'In this art they far surpass any people I have met.'

Clothing for men and women was basically the same: a cloak (brat) and mantle or long shirt (léine) worn without any other under or outer

Hibernian Male. & Female Costume.

Hibernian male and female costume. (*National Museum of Ireland*)

garment. The brat was four cornered, made of wool and fastened at the shoulder or breast by a brooch. Dyeing was another task and in old texts the most frequently mentioned colours are purple and crimson. Others were blue, yellow and black, as well as speckled and striped patterns. The mantle, also woolen, had a crios (girdle or belt) made of leather or woven from strands of wool of several colours. The belt was used to carry a purse or weapon. Decorating the clothing was not considered a menial task so Dervorgilla would probably have helped in the weaving of the sometimes elaborate fringes of the cloak, a forerunner to the embroidery done by royalty and ladies-in-waiting. Certainly, in later years, she proved herself to be a woman of great taste and artistic discernment.

Dervorgilla's life was played out against a background of extraordinary violence. It would be difficult to imagine a more turbulent period in Irish history than that of the twelfth century. The laws of succession ensured that violence lay at the heart of the family. Tighernan was called the One-Eyed King of Breifne, possibly as a result of losing an eye in battle or, more likely, from an attempted blinding. The chieftains were constantly at war to expand their kingdoms, raiding and counter-raiding each other's territory.

In the larger picture, the absence of a High King meant there was no central power in Ireland. Throughout the first half of the century the office of the High Kingship was an extremely contentious issue. At one stage, there were as many as three contenders in the field, leading to the formation of alliances and factions amongst the chieftains in support of each.

These wars and battles were ferocious affairs. The warriors rode bareback into the fray with loud cries. Their arms were the spear and that most deadly of weapons, the swinging axe. The Normans later feared the Irish axe and the skill with which it was wielded. It was recorded of John the Wode that 'with his axe of hard iron he chopped the thigh off to the ground'. He went on to kill some nine or ten Normans in the same battle. Groups of Irish foot soldiers immediately beheaded those who had been thrown to the ground. In one battle, Giraldus recounts that more than 200 heads were laid at the victor's feet, namely in this instance, Dermot MacMurrough, who shouted with joy when he recognised an enemy's face and brandished the head aloft. To add to the mayhem it was customary during a raid to drive off the herds of cattle, which were the chief's source of wealth, maiming and killing them.

Horseman. (*National Museum of Ireland*)

Tighernan and Dermot were warrior kings whose priorities were their fellow warriors, their horses, and their weapons. War and training for war were paramount. Women's status was very much inferior. David Starkey observed that women in the Tudor era were 'mere breeding machines', particularly in royal circles. It is clear that Tighernan had at least one other wife, as Dervorgilla could not have been the mother of his son Aedh, killed in battle in 1124. Divorce and short-term unions were common. One wife was considered to be the chief wife and this would appear to have been the position of Dervorgilla.

She had married a man who was almost continually engaged in warring throughout his long rule. In 1127, Turlough O'Connor, with his eye on the High Kingship raided Meath and banished Dervorgilla's father.

Tighernan submitted to O'Connor and as a reward received a share of the Kingdom of Meath. This was just a few years after Dervorgilla's father had supported him as King of Breifne. This pattern of shifting alliances and loyalties based on whatever served his own needs continued for the rest of his life. While he sometimes fought with, and sometimes against the Ua Maeleachlainn of Meath and Turlough O'Connor, he was at all times in constant opposition to Dermot MacMurrough, King of Leinster.

Dermot MacMurrough was the son of Donnchadh MacMurrough, King of Uí Ceinnsealaigh, who was killed by the Norse of Dublin when Dermot was five years old. According to Giraldus the citizens of Dublin buried a dead dog with his body as a gesture of contempt. Following his brother's death in 1126 Dermot became King of Uí Ceinnsealaigh, at the age of sixteen.

We first hear of Dermot two years later, when Turlough, on his continued quest for the High Kingship, deposes him and sets up his own son Conor as King of the Uí Ceinnsealaigh. To consolidate the position, Turlough, joined by Tighernan O'Rourke, advanced into Leinster, raiding and pillaging. Large numbers of cattle were destroyed and maimed. While this was standard practice, the extremes of cruelty and extent of numbers involved provoked the *Annals* to comment, 'The illfame of that hosting rested on Tighernan O'Rourke.' That raid of 1128 caused lasting enmity between Dermot and Tighernan. Many years later, the author of

Cattle Raid. (*National Museum of Ireland*)

The Song of Dermot and the Earl, when writing about the elopement, says that Dermot:

> Only wished to the utmost of his power
> To avenge, if he could, the great shame
> Which the men of Leath-Cuinn wrought of old
> On the men of Leath-Mhogha in his territory.

It was also a portent for the future that shortly afterwards Dermot made a treaty with Dervorgilla's father, Murchadh O'Maeleachlainn, with a promise to aid him in future struggles. This promise he kept in 1138 when they joined forces against the combined armies of Turlough O'Connor, Tighernan O'Rourke, and Donough O'Carroll. No battle took place. The armies remained encamped for a week, facing one another before dispersing. It showed the growing power of MacMurrough as well as the start of close ties between him and the O'Maeleachlainn family. Was it at this time that Dervorgilla began to resent and hate Tighernan for his disloyalty to her father and to feel gratitude to Dermot for his help? She was about thirty then and Dermot twenty-eight.

The following years were stormy in the extreme. War prevailed on all fronts. Dermot, having regained his throne, showed his determination to secure it by disposing of no fewer than seventeen of his rivals either by killing or blinding. Tighernan O'Rourke, who had succeeded in expanding his kingdom from its original size of Leitrim and Cavan to an area described in the *Annals* as stretching from Ballisodare Strand in Co. Sligo to Athboy in Co. Meath, and from the River Shannon to Oldbridge near Drogheda, was now under siege on three fronts. Firstly, he was engaged in quelling revolt among his own people in Conmaicne; secondly, he was attempting to maintain his influence in the Kingdom of Meath, and thirdly, he was struggling to retain his territories in North Connaught. Turlough O'Connor, the most powerful contender for the High Kingship, took Dervorgilla's father prisoner and gave the Kingdom of Meath to his son Conor. Within a year Conor was killed and Turlough delivered an almighty battle on the Meathmen so that the dead were numbered as the 'sands of the sea'. In 1144, in an effort to call a halt to the widespread bloodshed, the Church intervened and brought about a peace settlement. The peace was shortlived, because the *Annals* for 1145 make the graphic entry, 'great war, so that Ireland was a trembling sod'.

Matters got progressively tougher for Tighernan throughout the late 1140s. In a strong bid for the High Kingship, the King of Aileach in the north, Muircertach MacLochlainn, succeeded in gaining control of territories in the northern half of the country, forcing both Dermot MacMurrough and Tighernan O'Rourke to submit to him. Around the same time, Tighernan's own people of Conmaicne revolted against him and in an about-turns, there was an attempt to kill him at the instigation of his former ally Turlough O'Connor. By 1152, the Conmaicne did free themselves of the hegemony of the O'Rourke dynasty when O'Connor, now allied with Dermot MacMurrough, burned O'Rourke's longfort on the west side of the Shannon. Tighernan was deposed and the Conmaicne were forced into submission to O'Connor. The loss of his lands was a low point for Tighernan, added to which, was the realisation that he now had no hope of expanding his power into north Connaught. He had been left out of the new division of Meath, which was now under the control of O'Connor, MacLochlainn and Dermot MacMurrough. It was at this point that Tighernan O'Rourke retreated to Lough Derg and while there, that the calamity of the elopement of his wife with Dermot MacMurrough occurred.

This was a shocking and deeply humiliating experience for Tighernan O'Rourke. As well as the sense of personal betrayal, there was the added bitterness that it was perpetrated by his enemy Dermot MacMurrough. Even in an era without the tabloid press, the story went the length and breadth of Ireland; the ignominy of his position was difficult for a proud man to bear. Giraldus, admittedly a biased reporter, states that it was the disgrace, rather than the loss of his wife, that grieved him more deeply. *The Song* describes his actions in the immediate aftermath:

> O'Rourke, much grieving
> To Connaught went in all haste
> To the King of Connaught he related all
> Bitterly he complained of the shame.

Nobody could have envisaged the importance of the train of events it helped set in motion. Why did Dervorgilla choose this moment to act when her husband was at his lowest ebb? There are no diaries from the twelfth century. We can only conjecture about her thoughts and feelings. The *Annals* make cryptic references and give very few clues. Only once do we hear her voice, and then at second hand, when the *Annals of Tighernach* make the brief but telling reference, that Dervorgilla had complained to her brother Maelsechlainn of 'some abuses done to her by her husband Tighernan O'Rourke'. O'Rourke was a violent man, though no more so than other warring chieftains. Had he been violent with Dervorgilla? For much of their marriage he had been in conflict with her family. Had she listened to the file and bard extol his bravery in some battle with her people? They would have been less than human if words had not been exchanged about his treatment of her family. In any case it seems safe to assume that it was not a love match. If she lived in fear of her husband this was the moment to act. Her brother, possibly enraged by her complaints of abuse and allied to Dermot in the recent upheavals, became actively involved in the abduction.

There was every reason for Dervorgilla to look kindly on Dermot especially in his dealings with her family. He was also closer to her in age; at forty-two, just two years her junior, while her husband was sixty. Contemporary accounts hint at a previous liaison. *The Song* says:

King Dermot often sent word
To the lady whom he so loved
By letter and by messenger
Often did the king send word
That she was altogether, in truth
The thing in the world that he most loved.

According to Geoffrey Keating, writing in 1630, 'There had been an illicit attachment between them many years previously.'

It is an interesting fact that in this same century over in France, in the court of Eleanor of Aquitane, troubadours were singing songs introducing the idea of love and joy. They idealised women, placed them on a pedestal and extolled their beauty. their white skin and beautiful eyes, and often sang of the pain of love and love at a distance. They filled an emotional gap in the arranged marriages of the times. In 1152, the same year that Eleanor's marriage was annulled, Dervorgilla, in a loveless marriage, eloped with Dermot MacMurrough. *The Song* captures the drama of the story. Dervorgilla sent a message:

> That she would let King Dermot know
> In what place he should take her
> Where she would be in concealment
> That he might carry her off

The Song is more cynical about Dermot:

> Dermot, King of Leinster
> Whom the lady loved so much
> Made pretence to her of loving
> While he did not love her at all

It then goes on to state that he wished only to take vengeance for past defeats at the hands of O'Rourke. Whatever the truth of Dermot's feelings, it seems obvious that he would relish the opportunity of this final humiliation of O'Rourke. And if Dervorgilla lived in fear of her husband, this was the moment to act.

Dermot journeyed with his men to O'Rourke's stronghold in Dromahaire, Co. Leitrim

> Where the lady had sent word
> She would be ready

Dervorgilla's ladies-in-waiting reputedly cried and screamed, perhaps to make it appear to be an abduction or perhaps because they were not informed of the secret assignation. This was high drama and romance but, on a practical level, Dervorgilla took her dowry of cattle and furniture with her. This fact, as well as the involvement of her brother, suggests it was an abduction with all parties willing. *The Song* catches the excitement and speed of the dash to safety:

> In this way Dermot the king
> Carried off the lady at this time
> King Dermot then brought the lady away with him
> Nor ever ceased marching

From there to the midst of Hy Kinnselagh.

On that long flight from Breifne to Ferns where Dermot had his strong-hold, Dervorgilla's mind must have been in emotional turmoil, filled with anticipation and excitement and incredulity at the bravery of her action, and satisfaction in her revenge on Tighernan's treachery to her family, mingled with fear of his retaliation. But in all of this it would have been impossible for her to envisage the train of events that would follow her elopement.

Immediately on his return to Dromahaire, a stunned Tighernan O'Rourke set out to see Turlough O'Connor. While they had recently been at war, he now submitted to Turlough in the hope that his former ally would come to his aid:

> To the King of Connaught he related all
> How the King of Leinster came upon him in such a manner
> Took his wife by force from him
> And placed her at Ferns for her abode
> To the King of Connaught of the outrage
> Bitterly he complained of the injury
> Very earnestly he besought him
> To make ready for him
> Some of his household and of his men
> So that he could avenge his shame.

Dervorgilla remained at Ferns for a year. Eventually Turlough was per-suaded to take Tighernan's cause on board. He marched on Dermot, seized Dervorgilla and her cattle and returned her to her husband. So ended the most dramatic phase of Dervorgilla's life. Dermot had six chil-dren, one of them a daughter called Dervorgil. Was she the natural child of Dermot and Dervorgilla? In fact there is no record of Dervorgilla's children. It is pretty certain that she was the mother of Tighernan's son Maelsechlainn as he bore her brother's name and also the mother of Aedh, the heir to Breifne, who was tragically killed in 1171.

In 1152, the same year as the elopement, the Church thought fit to hold a synod at Kells under Cardinal Paparo which condemned irregular unions and concubinage. Did these pronouncements from the Church have their effects on Dervorgilla? Certainly following her

Mellifont Abbey.
(*Department of
the Environment,
Heritage and Local
Government*)

return to Breifne, we only hear of Dervorgilla in relation to Church
matters.

In 1157 she attended the consecration of Mellifont Abbey in the
company of her husband. At this magnificent event, attended by many
of the kings of Ireland and some seventeen bishops, Dervorgilla, in gracious benefactress role, gave gifts of 'three score ounces of gold, a chalice
of gold for the altar of Mary and altar cloths for the nine altars that were
in the church'. Tighernan also gave gifts, though not as splendid as his
wife's, showing an independence of action on her part. She must have
spent some time preparing for this occasion, choosing a craftsman to
make the chalice and commissioning nuns to design and make the altar

cloths. As a lady of taste and beauty, Dervorgilla must have looked quite regal herself for this important event in a beautiful cloak and gold jewellery. Drama was provided at Mellifont when Donagh O'Maeleachlainn, a relation of Dervorgilla, was publicly excommunicated for offences against the Church. He had also been dethroned from the kingship of Meath and replaced by his brother Diarmuid. Tighernan, to his chagrin, learned that he was excluded once again from any power in Meath. No one at this consecration of the first Cistercian monastery in Ireland could have known that they were looking at the last great assembly of so many kings and bishops, the lay and clerical rulers of Gaelic Ireland. In a few short years the Norman invasion would change everything.

There were no ominous warnings of this momentous event. The kings and princes of Ireland continued in their incessant warring. In 1156, O'Rourke, hell-bent on revenge, raided Leinster to attack Dermot MacMurrough. Though this venture ended in failure, his clashes with Dermot would persist over the following years. Turlough O'Connor died the same year and he was succeeded by his son Ruairí. By 1159, competition between Ruairí O'Connor of Connaught and Murtagh MacLochlainn of Ulster for the high kingship had reached new heights. O'Rourke and MacMurrough found their natural positions in opposing one another with O'Rourke supporting O'Connor and MacMurrough allying himself with MacLochlainn. In 1161 O'Rourke, still trying to stake his claim to Meath invaded with O'Connor's help but they were repulsed by MacLochlainn. The intense rivalry came to a climax at the great battle of Ardee in 1165 when MacLochlainn and his north men routed O'Connor of Connaught with tremendous slaughter.

Now that MacLochlainn was the acknowledged High King, MacMurrough felt sufficiently strong in Leinster to embark on Church reform. His brother-in-law Lorcan O'Toole was consecrated Archbishop of Leinster, while a synod was held at Clane, Co. Kildare to deal with some Church abuses. In common with the O'Rourkes of Breifne, Dermot was a generous patron of the Church. In 1161, he had founded the Augustinian monastery at Ferns. He also founded the Cistercian abbey at Baltinglass, the convent of St Mary de Hogges near Dublin and the priory of All Hallows (site of Trinity College).

Dermot's supremacy in Leinster was to end suddenly, when his ally Muircertach MacLochlainn, was killed in battle in 1166. Ruairí

O'Connor seized his chance, set out for Dublin, and proclaimed himself High King of Ireland. Dermot fled to his stronghold at Ferns, pursued by O'Connor and significantly, Tighernan O'Rourke. Many of Dermot's followers deserted him and his house was set ablaze. He was forced to submit to the new High King and to give hostages. He was allowed to remain on his lands but was deposed as King of Leinster. These humiliations were not enough to satisfy Tighernan, who shortly afterwards marched once more against Dermot. Unable to rally allies Dermot fled, but this time it was across the sea to Wales to seek help from Henry II.

Dermott MacMurchada. (*National Museum of Ireland*)

The fateful step had been taken.

In August 1167, Dermot returned with a small band of Welsh knights and archers under a knight called Richard Godibert. He was able to reclaim his lands of Uí Ceinnsealaigh and, emboldened by this, tried to establish himself once more as King of Leinster. Ruairí O'Connor would have none of this and again accompanied by Tighernan O'Rourke, marched against him and put him to flight. Ten score heads of the defeated Leinster men were brought to the victors. So confident did O'Connor feel following this victory that he allowed Dermot to remain on his lands, taking two of his sons as hostages as a guarantee of future behaviour. O'Rourke accepted a hundred ounces of gold as his log-enech (or honour price) for the abduction of his wife Dervorgilla. Fifteen years on, Tighernan O'Rourke had clearly not forgiven nor forgotten.

Both O'Connor and O'Rourke proceeded back to their kingdoms, well satisfied with the outcome, believing that the vanquished Dermot would cause no further trouble. In less than a year MacMurrough was promising his foreign allies, in return for help,

> Whoever shall wish for land or peace
> Horses, trappings or chargers
> Gold or silver I shall give them
> A very ample pay.

In May of 1169, the invasion proper began with two landings in Bannow Bay in Co. Wexford of knights, horsemen and archers, a force of 600 men under Robert Fitzstephen and Maurice de Prendergast. Dermot, with 500 of his followers, joined them. From the outset the invaders were successful. Much has been written about the military superiority of the Norman soldiers, wearing coats of mail and helmets, carrying lances and shields, of the skill of their archers with their deadly iron-tipped arrows. The Irish, without armour, had spears, battleaxes, swords and slings. Despite their pride and bravery they were no match for the organised Normans. Their only superiority lay in numbers and it must have been astonishing for the Irish that such small bands of Normans could be so effective.

Ruairí O'Connor, seriously underestimating the danger even after Wexford had been taken, offered to restore Dermot to the kingship of

Bayeaux Tapestry.

Leinster on condition that he would not bring any more foreigners to Ireland. As a precaution, he took Dermot's son as a hostage. This was merely an interlude. There was no halting of the avalanche, with the arrival of Maurice Fitzgerald with more men and yet another landing in May 1170 under the leadership of Raymond le Gros. At the battle of Baginbun more than a 1,000 Irish were killed and wounded. Seventy of the leading citizens of Waterford were taken prisoner and brutally executed. When Strongbow arrived in August 1170 with the largest force to date, over 1,000 men, the stage was set for the taking of Waterford.

Strongbow was Richard Fitzgilbert de Clare, earl of Pembroke, so nick-named because of his skill as an archer. In his efforts to entice him to come to Ireland, Dermot promised Strongbow his daughter Aoife in marriage with the understanding that he would succeed to the kingship of Leinster on Dermot's death. Despite a fierce defence, Waterford fell, due to a combined attack by Raymond le Gros and Strongbow. Within days the marriage of Strongbow took place. Giraldus describes Aoife as being of 'exceeding beauty' and records of Strongbow, a widower of over fifty:

His complexion was somewhat ruddy, and his skin freckled; he had grey eyes, feminine features, a weak voice and short neck. For the rest he was tall in stature, and a man of great generosity and of courteous manner.

Strongbow's succession to the kingship of Leinster would be totally alien to the customary laws of succession in Ireland but this did not appear to weigh heavily on Dermot, so keen was he to extract revenge on his enemies, in particular Tighernan O'Rourke.

Giraldus also left this description of Dermot MacMurrough:

> Dermot was tall of stature and of stout build. A man of warlike spirit and a brave one in his nation, with a voice hoarse from frequent shouting in the din of battle. One who preferred to be feared rather than to be loved, who was obnoxious to his own people and an object of hatred to strangers. His hand was against every man, and every man's hand against his.

The Norman advance now set its sights on Dublin. Ruairí O'Connor mustered a huge army and with Tighernan O'Rourke accompanying him, also marched to Dublin. The Normans surrounded the city and before any battles could be fought, the Norse leaders of Dublin negotiated a truce. Disgusted by this, O'Connor and O'Rourke marched homewards. Clearly MacMurrough felt no compunction in dishonour-

Wedding of Strongbow, detail. (*National Museum of Ireland*)

ing the truce, for MacCarthaigh's book describes the fall of Dublin as follows:

> Mac Murchadha and the earl went with their knights to Dublin and they drove out all the Norse, the merchants and the inhabitants who were there, killed or drowned many women and men and youths, and carried off much gold and silver and apparel. The English earl left the care of these, as well as of the town, in the hands of Diarmuid Mac Murchadha to avenge the wicked slaying of his father by the people of Dublin.

MacMurrough, excited and exultant in victory, continued on his vengeful path and set off in pursuit of O'Rourke, plundering Meath and Breifne. The *Annals* state that he afterwards 'made a predatory incursion into Tir Briúin, and carried off many persons and cows to their camp'. But he did not find or meet O'Rourke. It was to be Dermot's last foray. Ruairí O'Connor, enraged by his actions, executed his hostage, Dermot's son Conor, who was described by the annalists as 'the noblest and most amiable youth in Leinster'.

Less than a year later, in May 1171, Dermot was also dead. He became ill following the death of his son and retired to his stronghold at Ferns. He was sixty-one years old. The *Annals* say he died of 'an intolerable and uncommon disease' and give the graphic description, 'he became putrid while living'. Medical opinion has suggested typhus or venereal disease but there is the possibility that he could have contracted leprosy from one of the Norman knights who had been on the crusades to the Holy Land. For posterity, he had earned the soubriquet, Diarmuid na nGall (Dermot of the Strangers) for his role in inviting the Normans to Ireland.

The *Annals of Loch Ce* recorded his death as follows:

> Diarmuid Mc Murchadha, King of the province of Laighin
> after spoiling many churches and territories died at Ferna
> without the body of Christ, without penitence, without making
> a will – through the merits of Colum-Cille and Finnen and
> the other saints whose churches he had spoiled.

O'Rourke was to die in a more dramatic way. Henry II, suspicious and alarmed at Strongbow's success, decided to come to Ireland to ensure his own dominance over a possible Norman lordship of Ireland. He arrived with a large army of knights, archers, and horses, and also came with Papal approval in the guise of protector and reformer of the Church. Strongbow surrendered his Irish conquests to Henry, who then allowed him to remain as King of Leinster. Henry made triumphal progress through the land, receiving the submission of the Norman lords and of many of the Irish Kings including that of Ruairí O'Connor and Tighernan O'Rourke. The fact that the Irish Kings were retaining possession of their lands made this submission appear to be a matter of less consequence than might be supposed. But then Henry granted the Kingdom of Meath to Hugh de Lacy, a Norman knight, who had also been appointed as the King's representative in Dublin. This was a bitter blow for Tighernan O'Rourke who objected strongly. Eventually a meeting between O'Rourke and de Lacy was arranged to take place at the Hill of the Ward in Athboy, Co. Meath.

Despite Giraldus's efforts to describe what happened at this meeting in a noble light, it was clearly a set-up. The plan had been laid for the slaying of O'Rourke. To add to the treachery (but unsurprisingly). a member of O'Rourke's own clan was also involved, one Donal O'Rourke. The account of the killing must have been described many times, as Giraldus, though not present as a witness, has it in precise detail. He makes much of a dream that a knight called Griffin had on the night preceding the meeting, wherein a fierce boar charged at Hugh de Lacy and Maurice Fitzgerald. Griffin saved them by killing the boar. This was interpreted as a portent of possible treachery by O'Rourke. Arrangements for the meeting were elaborate, with messengers going back and forth between the two groups, who remained at a distance from each other. Then a very small number from both camps met, the Normans carrying swords and the Irish axes. Griffin and seven other knights came close to the hill and made a pretence of practising for a tournament. Though O'Rourke and de Lacy parleyed for some time, no agreement was reached. O'Rourke, that wily experienced warrior, obviously grew suspicious and according to Giraldus left the meeting and 'pretended to go a little way to make water and signalled to his men to come up at once with the utmost speed'. He returned with 'a pale, drawn expression and long, hasty strides with his axe raised'. Fitzgerald drew his sword and managed to avoid O'Rourke's axe, which cut off the arm of the interpreter who had thrown himself in front of Fitzgerald.

While O'Rourke and Fitzgerald fought, De Lacy managed to escape. The Irish rushed up the hill armed with spears and axes but Griffin and his knights were ready for them on their horses. O'Rourke made an attempt to escape when three of his men brought up his horse. In the words of Giraldus, 'just as Ua Ruairc was mounting, Griffin rode quickly forward and transfixed with his lance both the horse and the rider who was mounting it', exactly as he had killed the wild boar in his dream. O'Rourke's men were routed across the plains. So died the mighty O'Rourke just a year after his enemy Dermot MacMurrough. He was about eighty but still amazingly strong and active.

His death is lamented in the *Annals of Tighernach*:

Tighernan Ua Ruairc, king of Breifne and Conmaicne
and the greater part of the province of Meath,
deedful leopard of the Gael,
Leath Cuinn's man of battle and lasting defence,
Erin's raider and invader,
surpasser of the Gael in might and abundance
was treacherously killed by Eoan Mer and Richard,
the son of the earl, and by Domnall, son of Annach Ua Ruairc,
at the Hill of the Ward, and his body was brought
to Dublin to be mangled and drawn asunder.

The *Annals of Ulster* add, 'He was beheaded also by them and his head and his body were carried ignominiously to Dublin. The head was raised over the door of the fortress – a sore miserable sight for the Gael. The body was hung in another place, with its feet upwards.' This was standard treatment for a so-called traitor. In the coming centuries, Tighernan would not be the only O'Rourke to have his head sent to an English King and spiked as an example to other would-be traitors.

Dervorgilla outlived both Dermot and Tighernan by over twenty years. There is very little record of her life in those years. In 1167, when Dermot first returned with his band of Normans and Tighernan accepted his fine of 100 ounces of gold from Dermot for the abduction of 1152, Dervorgilla was busy at the monastic city of Clonmacnoise. She had continued to be a patron of the Church, no doubt making many pilgrimages to Mellifont and Clonmacnoise. At Clonmacnoise, among its many churches, stood O'Rourke's tower, built by Dervorgilla's husband's ancestor Fergal O'Rourke, King of Connaught, in the tenth century. When Fergal died in 966 he was buried in the O'Rourke family tomb within the confines of Clonmacnoise. The Nun's church had also been built in the tenth century, presumably to house an order of nuns. Dervorgilla took a particular interest in this building, which is regarded as one of the finest examples of Hiberno-Romanesque architecture. She added an elaborately carved chancel arch and doorway which are considered to be two of the most beautiful and noteworthy features at Clonmacnoise.

Following that endeavour of 1167, there is no further mention of Dervorgilla until her death in 1193. As for all the women of her time, hearing of the loss of a family member was a regular occurrence. Her brother Maelseachlainn, close friend and confidante, died in 1155, three years after assisting her in the elopement, 'of a poisonous drink in the thirtieth year of his age in the flood of his prosperity and reign'. In 1162, one of her sons, who was also called Maelseachlainn, 'Royal heir of Breifne, lamp of the chivalry and hospitality of Leath-Cuinn' was slain by Donal O'Rourke, the same Donal who would betray her husband. Again, in the absence of diaries or written accounts, we can only surmise at her grief on the death of another son, Aedh, in 1171. Later that year she learned of the death of Dermot MacMurrough. When her husband was slain in 1172 she could only look on as Donal O'Rourke took over the kingship of Breifne. Donal's reign did not last very long for he was killed a year later by the aes grada of Tighernan O'Rourke. His limbs were sent to Ruairí O'Connor, who nailed them to the top of his castle at Tuam. By 1186 her grandson Aedh was the new King of Breifne but again it was short-lived. Following his death in 1187, Ualgarg, son of Cathal Uí Ruairc, succeeded to the Kingship. She witnessed the shrinking of the kingdom from the midlands into what is now Leitrim, under the advancing power of Hugh de Lacy.

It was in this reduced kingdom of Breifne, probably at the O'Rourke stronghold in Dromahaire that she spent her remaining years. She found comfort in prayer and making pilgrimages. It was on one of those pilgrimages to Mellifont, that she died in 1193, at the age of eighty-four. The *Annals of the Four Masters* record, 'Dervorgilla, wife of Tighernan O'Rourke and daughter of O'Maoileachlainn died in the monastery of Droicheadh Atha in the eighty-fifth year of her life.' She is buried at Mellifont.

The twelfth century saw a convulsive change in the affairs of Ireland.

Nuns' Chapel, Clonmacnoise. (*Department of the Environment, Heritage and Local Government*)

When the century began, Ireland was Gaelic with Brehon laws, kings, chieftains, customs and a Gaelic way of life. At the end of the century, many of the Irish chieftains had been dispossessed of their lands, and Norman lords had introduced motte-and-bailey castles, a feudal system of tenantry and a form of centralised government. Regarding the rights of succession, the Irish system would be replaced by the English law of primogeniture, where the first born had the right to succeed, but the changes would continue over hundreds of years. Dermot MacMurrough, Tighernan O'Rourke and his wife Dervorgilla had played a significant role in this cataclysmic change.

The Story of Brian O'Rourke
(Brian of the Ramparts) 1564-1591

While the Norman Invasion established English claims to lordship over Ireland, the reality was that for the following 300 years real power remained with the Anglo-Irish and Gaelic lords. The Earls of Kildare, the Fitzgeralds, ruled as deputies of the English King, representing his power in Ireland, but their power was mostly restricted to the Pale. This was an area stretching from Dundalk to Dublin and inland for some twenty to thirty miles. These Anglo-Irish lords, while professing loyalty to the English King, valued their independence in Ireland. The Gaelic chieftains ruled as complete autocrats in their territories, retaining their laws and customs. This was certainly the case in Breifne where the O'Rourkes continued to rule in the centuries following the arrival of the Normans.

Little had changed when Brian na Murtha (Brian of the Ramparts) became Chief of Breifne in 1564. His inauguration followed the murder of his two brothers: Hugh Gallda at Leitrim Castle and Hugh Buidhe at Ballintogher. The suspicion was that they were slain to facilitate his accession. The *Annals of the Four Masters* state that they were slain 'by their own people' and add, 'it was rumoured that it was for him [Brian] that this foul deed was committed though he had no personal share in perpetrating it'. These killings ended almost thirty years of civil war between various families of the O'Rourkes.

In the Gaelic tradition, a poem was written to celebrate his succession to the chieftainship. Knowing the satirical powers of the poet it can be interpreted in different ways:

> Well is the rapture of eulogy due
> To him in whom treachery never could lurk
> Whose promise is sacred, whose friendship is true
> The glory of Feargna, the gallant O'Rourke

The same poem gives a description of Breifne which is recognisable today:

> O Breifne, dear land of the mountain and vale
> Where the heifers stray merrily all the long year
> How fragrant thy moorlands in summers fresh gale
> How green in its showers thy meadows appear

At the beginning of his rule, O'Rourke must have felt himself to be in a position of great power. He had many castles to defend his kingdom, one at Dromahaire, another at Newtown and a third on the shores of Lough

O'Rourke's Hall. (*National Library of Ireland*)

Gill. There was also a mighty castle at Leitrim built by his father Brian Ballach O'Rourke in 1540, the last castle of the O'Rourkes. There still remained a crannóg (island fortress) in Glencar Lake. The remains of the large banqueting hall in the castle of Dromahaire suggest that it had been a castle of considerable size. Hospitality was highly prized among the Gaelic chieftains and another poem, written in Irish and later translated by Dean Swift, pays tribute to the generosity of the O'Rourkes as hosts:

O'Rourke's noble fare
Will ne'er be forgot
By those who were there
Nor those who were not
His revels to keep
We sup and we dine
On seven score sheep
Fat bullocks and swine.

Brian O'Rourke was ruling in uneasy times. Following the crushing of the rebellion of the Fitzgeralds of Kildare, who had represented the power of the English monarchy in Ireland, there was a new determined

Feast. (*National Library of Ireland*)

effort by Henry VIII to bring Ireland into submission. O'Rourke would spend his life in fierce resistance to the advance of Tudor rule. To that end he remained in readiness with more than a 1,000 Scots mercenaries in his service. These were the Gallowglasses who had originally come from Scotland in the late 1300s. The McCabes were the hereditary Gallowglass family who served the O'Rourkes. The Gallowglass soldiers were equipped with helmets and coats of mail. Their standard weapon was a heavy battleaxe with a six-foot handle. Other families who served O'Rourke in times of war were the McLoughlins, McMorrices and the Clantrynan. The Irish troops (kern) were foot soldiers without armour and carried light weapons. The marshy, wooded and mountainous nature of his territory rendered it almost impregnable to attack. O'Rourke could afford to feel remote from the centres of power in Dublin. But the fact that his kingdom was the western 'Gap of the North', through which Scots mercenaries could travel into Connaught in search of hire, made Breifne a thorny issue for the English administration.

War was an expensive business, so the Crown hoped to subdue Connaught by persuading the native chieftains to surrender their lands to Queen Elizabeth and to receive them back by grant while promising loyalty to the Crown. The task of imposing English law on Connaught began in earnest when Sir Henry Sidney became Lord Deputy in 1570. The native chieftains would strongly resist any plans to surrender their lands and the fond hopes for a peaceful settlement resulted instead in thirty years of rebellion and bloodshed, especially so in the case of Brian O'Rourke.

When Sir Sidney commenced the process of English administration by dividing the province into shires or counties – Mayo, Galway, Clare, Roscommon and Sligo – Leitrim is noticeably absent. It retained this separate independent character to the end of the sixteenth century, due in part to its geographical fastness, but in particular to the character of Brian O'Rourke. His immense pride and sense of lineage and position is clear from the many comments made about him by English officials. Sir Sidney, writing about O'Rourke says, 'I found him the proudest man I have ever dealt with in Ireland.' Sir Nicholas Malby, the governor of Connaught, calls him 'the proudest man living the earth' and Sir Richard Bingham, who became the next governor and arch-enemy of O'Rourke, describes him as 'a proud beggar who thinks that even the Queen is afraid of him'. By the late 1580s, most of the chieftains, such as O'Connor

Sligo, McWilliam Burke of Mayo and other chieftains had made their submission to the Queen, O'Rourke still remained aloof.

Malby lost his patience; he attacked and captured O'Rourke's castle at Leitrim and plundered the property. This action had the desired effect; O'Rourke submitted and he received his castle back by grant. As a gesture of goodwill and in the hope of maintaining his loyalty, he was knighted. He was now Sir Brian O'Rourke. It was a superficial exercise, for O'Rourke held on to his force of Gallowglasses and was soon in revolt again.

O'Rourke was alarmed by the inroads of English laws, especially in the areas of title and succession. He would hold his lands but as a subject of the Queen. The Desmond rebellions in Munster had added the extra ingredient of religion, the rule of a Protestant Queen in a Catholic country. In 1580 he took up arms and in alliance with O'Donnell of Tirconnell, led a rebellion in the north-west. O'Rourke's method of warfare was of a guerrilla nature: raiding and pillaging territories and then retiring to the woods and fastnesses of Breifne. The attacks were against those chieftains who had submitted and now refused to join in the struggle. In one of the raids near Athlone many of Malby's soldiers were killed.

Malby had been kept busy in Munster but in August 1580 he set out to seek revenge. O'Rourke, on hearing this, sent his women and children across the mountain of Sliabh-an-Iarainn for safety, demolished his Leitrim Castle and withdrew. Malby rebuilt the castle in spite of the difficulty of having to draw lime from eight miles away. In this work, he was helped by O'Rourke's nephew, another Brian, who hoped to become the next chief of Breifne. Malby placed guards to protect the castle and boasted in a letter to England that O'Rourke had fled from him with 1,200 men. He neglects to add that later O'Rourke laid siege to the castle, forcing the guards to withdraw.

The following year, with a promise of 600 extra Gallowglasses from Tirlough Lynagh O'Neill of Ulster, O'Rourke planned to continue his campaign of resistance.

To prevent his castles being occupied by the English, he demolished his castles at Dromahaire and Newtown as they were too close to the garrison town of Sligo. Malby retaliated by convincing 300 Gallowglasses to abandon O'Rourke and fight for O'Connor Sligo instead. O'Rourke led his army into Annally (Longford), burned the country and carried off 1,000 cattle. Warfare for the chieftains had changed little since pre-Norman days. In a shrewd move, showing his understanding of the fierce internecine rivalry of the Irish clan, Malby ordered O'Rourke's nephew Brian, who had now been appointed sheriff of Sligo, to keep his uncle in order. In a show of force, the sheriff advanced into Breifne with an army and when he was withdrawing with great spoils, his men were attacked by O'Rourke's men and many of them were killed.

By this time O'Rourke's ally O'Donnell had submitted, making it difficult for O'Rourke to stand alone. He reluctantly agreed to a one-year truce and insisted that submission would be on his terms. It was during this year, 1583, that the county of Leitrim was defined. Towards the end of the year, Malby, fearing another revolt by O'Rourke, hired 500 Gallowglasses and sent the Earl of Thomond, the Baron of Leitrim and Captain Brabazon with 600 men to the borders of Breifne to confer with O'Rourke. In this threatening atmosphere, the truce was extended for a further two years.

The end of the two-year truce coincided with the appointment of a new Lord Deputy, Sir John Perrott and a new Governor of Connaught, Sir Richard Bingham. Both of these men would play significant roles in the affairs of Brian O'Rourke. From the start, there was jealousy and hostility between Perrott and Bingham. O'Rourke would unwittingly become involved in the mesh of Tudor court intrigue.

For the moment however, there was an uneasy peace. The apparent solution to the problem of Connaught was the settlement called The Composition of Connaught. This entailed an inquisition held by commissioners to estimate the quantity of land held by the chieftains in their various territories. An appropriate rent for the Queen was calculated and then the lands were regranted back to the chieftains with certain conditions.

On 26 September 1585, Sir Richard Bingham arrived in Dromahaire to hold an inquisition into the affairs of Breifne. The resultant agreement was considered by the authorities to be generous to Brian O'Rourke.

In return for his submission to the Queen, O'Rourke would retain his castles at Dromahaire, Newtown and Leitrim. Rent was fixed at 10s per quarter (a quarter was 120 acres) and it was estimated that he held 129 quarters of which 60 were in free demesne, which would not be subject to rent. He would hold his castles and lands. He would furnish horsemen and footmen to all hostings by the Governor in the prov-

Sir Richard Bingham. (*National Portrait Gallery, London*)

ince. In addition he would receive rent of 13*s* 4*d* per quarter out of 545 quarters of his freeholders' lands. All rents were annual fixed rents. More ominously for the future success of the agreement, it was stated that the 'customary election and division of lands occasioning great strife shall be utterly abolished in O'Rourke's country'. This meant the abolition of the Gaelic system of landownership and succession of title, and the introduction of English administration. By signing the agreement, O'Rourke had given away his rights and privileges as Chief of Breifne.

This was clearly too humiliating for an extremely proud O'Rourke to bear.

Within a year, O'Rourke had allowed the Composition rent to lapse and Bingham complained bitterly to Perrott. Bingham sought permission to attack O'Rourke, which Perrott would not give. The clash in strategy between the two men resulted in Bingham being recalled to London in 1587.

During Bingham's absence, O'Rourke, sensing that he had the unspoken support of the Lord Deputy, succeeded in convincing Perrott to reduce his rent by £100. He celebrated Christmas at Dromahaire, and it was in connection with these festivities that a curious incident occurred. It was in the nature of a pageant. There are three versions

Queen Elizabeth I.
(*National Portrait Gallery, London*)

of this event but the essential elements remain the same. Sir William Fitzwilliam, who became Lord Deputy after Perrott, reported that O'Rourke, having found an image in a church of a tall woman, wrote the name Elizabeth across the breast. While he reviled it with insults, his Gallowglasses hacked it with their axes. Then it was tied to a horse's tail and dragged through the mud. John Ball recounts witnessing in O'Rourke's country an image of a woman carved in a block and was told by the natives that it represented 'an old calliagh [hag] from across the water who refused a carpenter milk'. Later he was told it was an image of the Queen. The third version, by John Bingham, recounts 'a picture of the Queen with a pin in the belly of it which O'Rourke had dragged at a horse's tail calling it an old calliagh from across the water'. Whatever the truth or exaggerations of this story it was to have grave repercussions both for O'Rourke and Lord Deputy Perrott. It was one of the charges at their subsequent trials for treason a few years later. Perrott was tried for having taken no action when the incident had been reported and O'Rourke for insulting the Queen.

O'Rourke's hatred of the Queen was rooted in religion. The State Papers abound in complaints about O'Rourke, 'The Romish religion he holds for his only quarrel' and 'Friars practise with O'Rourke'. In 1579 his brother Conn, a Franciscan friar, was hanged. The O'Rourkes had long associations with the Franciscans. Brian's grandparents Owen and Margaret O'Rourke had founded the Franciscan monastery at Creevelea in Dromahaire in 1508. It is considered to be the most beautiful of all medieval Franciscan sites in Ireland and destined to become the last monastery set up before the dissolution of the monasteries under Henry VIII. Over the years, the O'Rourkes had been generous patrons of the Church, such as the monastery and college founded at Fenagh by St Cailin. In 1526 Brian's father Brian Ballach had an ornate cover made for a shrine (designed to hold a bible) while another O'Rourke commissioned a copy of the famous *Book of Fenagh*. There is a grudging description of Brian O'Rourke as 'being somewhat learned but of an insolent and proud nature' in a *Treatise of Ireland*. He lived his life according to the Brehon laws in that while he was legally married to Lady Mary Burke and they had a son Teige, the chieftainship would go to his older son Brian Oge, whose mother was Annabla, wife of a Sligo merchant John O'Crean. In later life, he married Lady Eleanor Butler, daughter of the Earl of Desmond, who died in childbirth after only a year of marriage.

When Bingham returned to Ireland in the spring of 1588 to learn of the desecration of the Queen's image and Perrott's failure to take any action, he set out to attack O'Rourke at his castle in Dromahaire. Forewarned, O'Rourke took flight into the dense woods of Breifne. Bingham reported on the matter to the Privy Council who ordered O'Rourke's arrest. Meanwhile, Perrott had been replaced by Sir William Fitzwilliam.

★ ★ ★ ★ ★

In the same year of 1588 dramatic event occurred which would seal the fate of Brian O'Rourke of Breifne. King Philip II of Spain, worried about the growing maritime power of England, launched an Armada of 130 ships against the heretic Queen Elizabeth I. After a disastrous encounter with the English fleet in the Channel, some of the ships tried to make their way back to Spain by sailing northwards around Scotland and then southwards by the west coast of Ireland. Storms and high seas resulted in many of the ships being wrecked on the Scottish

Spanish Armada.

and Irish coasts. Others were forced to seek shelter on Irish shores. For the English administration in Ireland it seemed as if their fears of a possible Spanish invasion were being realised. Lord Deputy Fitzwilliam acted speedily. His brief to Sir Thomas Norris, Sir George Boucher and others in his command was to take 'all the hulls of ship, stores, treasure into your hands and to apprehend and execute all Spaniards found there of what quality soever'. Furthermore, a proclamation was issued, 'upon pain of death that any man, who had or kept Spaniards, should deliver them to the Provost Marshal or else be reputed a traitor'.

The shocking treatment of the Spanish, who struggled ashore from their ships, demonstrates both the paranoid anxiety of the English administration of a possible Spanish foothold in Ireland and also the state of fear and subjugation of the native Irish. It has been estimated that about 5,000 Spanish lost their lives. Many drowned when their ships broke up in storms off the coast; other ships foundered on the rocks as they tried to anchor. Many of the unfortunate Spaniards who scrambled onto the rocks and beaches were butchered by locals who stripped them of their clothes and money. The Spanish noblemen had concealed money and jewels in their clothing. Others who at first were sheltered, were handed over to the authorities after the proclamation had been issued. Sir Richard Bingham, Governor of Connaught, supervised the execution of 300 miserable Spaniards in Galway. There were many atrocities on the Irish side, such as the massacre of 100 Spaniards on Clare Island by Dubhdara Rua O'Malley. Near Killala, William Burke captured seventy-two Spaniards, while one Melaghlan McCabb, a Scot, waded into the water and axed to death some eighty hapless and helpless Spaniards as they tried to come ashore.

From Sligo, George Bingham, Sheriff of Sligo, sent an urgent letter to his brother Richard, the governor of Connaught, that 'three Spanish ships were cast upon the coast in Co. Sligo of which one thousand, eight hundred men had drowned' and made the boast that 'seven score who came ashore had been executed by myself'. He is referring here to the three Spanish ships shipwrecked at Streedagh Strand in Co. Sligo, during a violent storm. An English official, in his report on the event states, 'I numbered in one strand of less than five miles in length above one thousand corpses of men which the sea had driven upon the shore.' One of the ships was the *San Juan de Sicilia* and on board was Captain

Streedagh, Co. Sligo. (*Photograph: Tommy Weir*)

Francisco Cuellar. He was one of a band of about twenty who managed to survive the shipwreck, avoid the English sword or capture, and escape being killed by the local inhabitants.

Francisco Cuellar, fortunately for history, wrote an account of his time in Ireland. It is against the background of the ruthless treatment of the Spanish by a nervous English administration that the actions of Brian O'Rourke appear so merciful. No doubt he saw the possibility of a grateful King of Spain sending help for his own struggle, but he was also completely sympathetic to Catholic Spain's action against the Protestant Queen Elizabeth. In a vivid description, Cuellar tells of his miraculous luck, that despite being unable to swim, he was washed ashore clutching a piece of timber, and remained hidden amongst the rushes in the sand dunes for some time. He describes the terrible scene at the beach at Streedagh where ravens and wild dogs fed on the corpses, and when he made his way inland, of coming across a small church, believed to be the abbey of Staad, where he tells, 'I went to the church which was forsaken, the images of the saints burned and destroyed, and within, were twelve Spaniards hanged by the English

41

Lutherans, who were prowling around in quest of us in order to finish with all who had escaped from the disasters of the sea.' He was joined by two Spanish soldiers who had been stripped naked. As they made their way slowly inland, they met with a mixture of brutality and rough justice. They were attacked by four men, who were stopped by their leader from taking Captain Cuellar's clothes, who then directed them to his village. On the way, they were attacked again by two men who tore off Cuellar's clothing and stole a gold chain and forty-five gold crowns. At the request of a young girl, who was with them, they returned his clothes. Later, a young boy arrived with milk, butter and oaten bread. This was a welcome respite from the diet of berries and watercress. The next attack, by a group of young men, left him beaten and stripped finally of his clothes. To cover himself, he plaited rushes and ferns together to form a skirt. He reached a group of small huts and found three more Spaniards. There also, he met a young man who, speaking in Latin, gave them the wonderful news that six leagues away, there was a friendly country that belonged to a great lord, who was a good friend to the King of Spain. In Captain Cuellar's words:

> God was pleased to bring us to a land of some safety where we found a village belonging to better people, Christian and kindly. In that village there were seventy Spaniards and the women and children cared for them most charitably. The chief was not there at this time. Although he is a savage, he is a very good Christian and an enemy of the heretics and always fights against them. His name is Lord de Ruerge.

Brian O'Rourke provided a safe haven for the desperate Spaniards both at his own castle and in the Rosclogher castle of his sub-king Mac Clancy. Francisco de Cuellar gives an interesting description of the people:

> ...they live in huts made of straw. The men have big bodies, their features and limbs are well-made, and they are as agile as deer. They eat but one meal at night, and their ordinary food is bread of an oaten kind and butter. They drink sour milk as they have no other beverage, but no water, although it is the best in the world. On feast-days they eat meat, half-cooked, without bread or salt. They dress in tight breeches and goatskin jackets cut very short but very big. Overall they wear a blanket or cloak and they wear their hair down to their eyes. They are good walkers and have great endurance.

Describing the women he writes:

> Most of the women are pretty but ill-dressed. They wear nothing but a
> shift and a cloak over it, and a linen cloth much folded on their heads
> and tied in front. They are hard workers and good housewives after their
> fashion. These people call themselves Christians, hear Mass and follow the
> usages of the Church.

It is clear that Captain Cuellar created his own aura of interest and was a
great charmer. He paints an amusing and delightful scene when he writes:

> The Chieftain's wife was exceedingly comely. I told her and the other
> womenfolk their fortunes as they sat in the sun. I told them a hundred
> thousand nonsensical things at which they were mightily pleased. But day
> and night both men and women followed me incessantly, asking me to
> have their fortunes told.

He reveals a good picture of the general mayhem of the people at times:

> ...their great bent is to be robbers and to steal from one another, so that
> not a day passes without a call to arms among them. For when a man
> of one village learns that there are cattle or anything else in another
> village, they go at once armed at night and shouting war-cries to kill
> one another. When the English learn which village has gathered in the
> most cattle, they swoop down on it and take it all away. These people
> have no other help than to fly to the mountains with their wives and
> flocks, for they possess no other property, neither household staff nor
> clothes. They sleep on the ground upon rushes freshly cut and full of
> water or else frozen stiff.

His description matches that of a contemporary report by an English
official, Dymmok, who describes the Irish as, 'good horsemen, frank,
ireful, able to endure great pains'. He refers to their 'delight in war' and
great hospitality. He also calls them Papists, 'deep dissemblers, quick-wit-
ted' and says 'they have clear complexions, are tall and corpulent-bodied'.
Captain Cuellar was aware of Spanish indebtedness to the chieftains and
the people of Breifne and he soberly states 'had it not been for these
people not one of us would now be alive'.

It did not take long for George Bingham, Sheriff of Sligo, to send an urgent report to his brother Sir Richard saying that, 'Certain Spaniards, being stripped, were relieved by O'Rourke, apparelled and new furnished with weapons.' The fear of an Irish and Spanish alliance is evident from the swift action of Lord Deputy Fitzwilliam, who personally led an army of 1,800 men into Breifne and laid siege to MacClancy's castle at Rosclogher, where De Cuellar and his companions were then being sheltered. MacClancy, on hearing of the advance of such a large force, fled to the hills with his household. De Cuellar and his small band of comrades volunteered to remain behind and promised to defend the castle to the death, saying, 'it was better to die with honour rather than to wander naked and barefoot in the freezing snow'.

They remained in the castle, refusing to surrender even under the blandishments of a promise of a safe passage back to Spain. De Cuellar was proved correct in his estimation of the risk factor, because snow it did – great clouds of drifting snow – but now the snows worked to their advantage because it was this snow that forced the lifting of the siege after seventeen days. He wrote, 'God was pleased to help us and to deliver us from our enemies by means of terrible storms and heavy snows that came upon them in such manner that they were forced to raise the siege and to march away.' De Cuellar eventually made his way northwards, where he was helped by the Bishop of Derry, Redmond O'Gallagher. De Cuellar sailed to Scotland and after a wait of some months, set sail for Spain in a rescue mission mounted by the Duke of Parma.

Meanwhile, Sir Richard Bingham was keeping the Lord Deputy well informed. He wrote, 'an Irish friar is gone to O'Rourke with letters from the King of Spain giving thanks for his services to the dispersed ships of the Armada. O'Rourke is daily visited with letters and messages from all parts of Ireland.' Rumours were spreading and suspicion was running high. Retribution was to begin for O'Rourke.

★ ★ ★ ★ ★

In 1588 O'Rourke married the Earl of Desmond's daughter Eleanor. In the same year she travelled to Dublin to ask the Lord Deputy not to send sheriffs into her husband's country, and not surprisingly she had been refused. The following year Bingham reported to the Lord Deputy, 'O'Rourke's wife, that honest woman, is deceased in childbirth.'

O'Rourke appeared to be in no doubt why it happened. He complained to the Lord Deputy that Sir Richard Bingham attacked him in Dromahaire followed by another attack by Ulick Burke (Clanricarde), 'all to surprise him, at which time the Lady O'Rourke was so sore frightened that she died'.

Lord Deputy Fitzwilliam and other members of the English administration disapproved of Bingham's methods of fire and sword, which was resulting in rebellion among the chieftains of Connaught. Jealousy and intrigue were rife, and there were those who hoped to have Bingham dismissed on grounds of mismanagement and evidence that his family were keen to share in the spoils of Connaught. One of them, Sir Robert Dillon, secretly encouraged O'Rourke to rebel and gave the understanding that the Lord Deputy would turn a blind eye. O'Rourke supported the other rebels, the Burkes and the O'Flahertys of Connaught, who resented their subjugation under the iron hand of Governor Sir Richard Bingham. He arranged to have his son Brian Oge of the Battleaxes O'Rourke, smuggled out of Oxford where he was being educated in the English way. O'Rourke was furious over the burning of Dromahaire and the killing of a relation by the Sherriff of Sligo. He was more than ever strongly resistant to the idea of sheriffs having any power in his country.

Meanwhile, Fitzwilliam came to Connaught to set up a Commission for the Pacification of Connaught. It sat for twenty days but failed to reach a settlement with the O'Flahertys. Brian Oge O'Rourke, newly released from Oxford and with all the energy of youth, took a force of forty horsemen and 400 Gallowglasses to the Ballymote headquarters of Richard Bingham's brother George, and drove off 3,000 cattle and a 1,000 mares. Richard forcefully told the Commission that O'Rourke 'must be suppressed and resisted in time else he will grow stronger and attempt greater things'.

He swiftly ordered O'Rourke's brother-in-law Ulick Burke, Earl of Clanricarde, to attack O'Rourke. Clanricarde marched from Elphin to Ballinafad where he was informed by the Sheriff of Sligo, John Byrmingham, that O'Rourke was at Dromahaire. He set out, travelling by night, to surprise O'Rourke but at daybreak his troops were observed by some of O'Rourke's followers, who rushed to inform O'Rourke. At first hurried preparations were made to defend but on realising the superiority of the forces against him, O'Rourke decided to vacate the town of Dromahaire. Clanricarde pursued but failed to catch up with him. Morrough na Mort, whom O'Rourke had hired with a band of 200 mercenaries, became involved in a fight in which he lost an eye, while some of his force escaped through the bogs. This was the attack mentioned by O'Rourke when referring to the death of his wife in childbirth.

Lord Deputy Fitzwilliam decided to try pacification once more and refused to allow Bingham to attend the hearings in Galway, on the grounds that the natives would not speak freely in his presence. Bingham, knowing that his position as Governor was in question, wrote letters furiously attacking O'Rourke. He called him 'an arch traitor – the nurse of all mischief'. He states that 'of all these broils, that cowardly traitor O'Rourke, is the only stirrer whose power is so great that with two hundred Englishmen I will undertake to banish him'. To his chagrin, he was ignominiously summoned to Dublin and spent six weeks there, answering charges that the Connaught Chieftains had made against him.

Fitzwilliam went to Sligo and sent three of his commissioners, among them Sir Robert Dillon, to the borders of Breifne to negotiate with O'Rourke. O'Rourke made it clear he would not attend talks at which Bingham or any of his agents were present. He would go to Dublin under 'safe conduct' and deal only with the Lord Deputy. He demanded that no sheriffs be placed in his country and said he would make no restitution for the damage he had caused in the war, unless he were first compensated for the harm inflicted on him. Fitzwilliam returned to Dublin with a promise from O'Rourke that he would go to Dublin to make peace. No doubt Bingham was furious over the flouting of his authority but Fitzwilliam was hopeful of a peace settlement.

Unfortunately for O'Rourke it was at this stage that the secret plots of some within the Dublin council began to unfold. He was not to know until it was too late, but he was being used as a tool by those who wished to get rid of Bingham, by allowing the revolts to continue. While Fitzwilliam waited for O'Rourke to attend him in Dublin, one of the plotters, Sir Robert Dillon, urged O'Rourke not to come and warned him not to trust Fitzwilliam. A meeting had been arranged and Fitzwilliam appointed Bishop Jones, Sir Thomas Le Strange, and Sir Robert Dillon to act as safe conductors to O'Rourke. They journeyed to Longford to meet O'Rourke and escort him to Dublin. Significantly, Sir Robert Dillon stayed behind in Dublin and made a visit to Charles Trevor who was a prisoner in Dublin Castle. Charles Trevor was a former spy of O'Rourke's who had stage-managed the escape of O'Rourke's son from Oxford. Dillon persuaded him to write a letter to O'Rourke warning him not to come to Dublin. The ploy worked because O'Rourke did not go to Longford to join his escort to Dublin to meet Lord Deputy Fitzwilliam. Hindsight would show that this was a serious mistake.

In England, Sir John Perrot, who had earlier shielded O'Rourke from Bingham, realised that O'Rourke could not hold out any longer. He sent two brothers, John and Patrick Garland, to visit O'Rourke in Dromahaire. They urged him to submit to the Lord Deputy before it was too late. Dillon sent word to O'Rourke not to trust Perrot. O'Rourke at last sensed that he was been duped but was undecided what action to take. He told the Garland brothers, 'I would you had come six or seven weeks sooner for then I had not done that which I have; but now I am so far gone as I cannot draw back again.' O'Rourke, obviously felt it was too late to change course but submission was not in the nature of this proud man; the passing of his power to sheriffs was a matter he refused to contemplate. He remained in revolt.

Brian Oge led a raid in Sligo and seized 800 cows and horses and killed twenty men in the forces of Sir George Bingham. Finally Lord Deputy Fitzwilliam gave the order to attack O'Rourke. Sir Richard, due to an illness, was forced to delegate this longed-for task to his brother George. A large force entered Breifne and spent a month pursuing the scorched-earth tactics of Bingham, burning and spoiling. They were helped by O'Rourke's nephews Donnell, son of Teige, and Hugh Oge son of Hugh Gallda, who had been murdered in O'Rourke's rise to power. The MacRannals, who were sub-chiefs of O'Rourke, cast their lot in with the Binghams. His old friend and ally McClancy stayed loyal and fought the forces of Sir George in the area around Dromahaire. Being overcome, he was forced to flee. Bingham described what happened. 'McClancy tried to save himself by swimming (he had jumped into a lake) but a shot broke his arm and a galloglass pulled him ashore'. He was beheaded on the spot and Bingham adds, 'He was the best killed man in Connaught for a long time. He was the most barbarous creature in Ireland and always had a hundred knaves about him.' O'Rourke retreated north to McSweeney na dTuath in Donegal and his son Brian Oge went to Fermanagh. Bingham reported that his country had been divided and:

> …all the principal septs have come in and given pledges to observe
> Her Majestie's peace and bound themselves that if O'Rourke continue
> his disloyalty they will treat him as a rebel. He will never recover his
> greatness for his country doth for the most part hate him, his tyrannies
> are so great.

While Sir Richard Bingham was well satisfied with the destruction of
Breifne, his spies kept a close watch on O'Rourke in Donegal.

Brian O'Rourke remained with McSweeney until the end of 1590,
considering his options. He decided to go to see King James VI of
Scotland. James was the son of Mary Stuart, the Catholic Queen of
Scotland, who had been executed by her cousin Queen Elizabeth.
Links with Scotland were close; apart from the recruitment of
Gallowglasses, there was also a busy trade between the two countries. Secretly O'Rourke harboured hopes of raising mercenaries to
continue his fight at home. At the very least he expected asylum and
perhaps intercession with the Queen. He arrived in February 1591 with
gifts of 'six faire Irish hobbies and fowre great dogges to be presented
to the king here'. Irish wolfhounds and horses were highly prized in
England and were often sent as presents. Again it would appear that
O'Rourke misjudged the politics of the situation. There had been a
thaw in English and Scottish relations with the signing of an alliance at
Berwick in 1584. Moreover James, who had been brought up in a strict
Calvinist tradition, was dependent on Elizabeth for an annual pension.
He refused to meet O'Rourke and consulted with the English ambas-
sador Robert Bowes who informed the Queen. She wrote a letter to
James, demanding O'Rourke's delivery as a traitor, calling him 'a pro-
fessed rebel and a most notable traitour towards us and our crowne of
Ireland having been … a rebellious subject against all forme of justice
these many years'.

When O'Rourke was arrested in Glasgow many of the citizens
protested, fearing a loss of trade with Ireland. It was to no avail and
O'Rourke was escorted to London and placed in the Tower to await his
trial for treason. It was an early case of extradition. In Dublin a report
was drawn up concerning O'Rourke, 'A trew reporte of some parte
of the tratorus actions and misdemenours committed of late yeares by

the Traytor Sir Brian O'Rourke, late of Leotrim, knighte.' Sir Richard Bingham was active in the matter, which was discussed by the council and Lord Deputy on 28 July 1591. From this the grand jury of Middlesex drew the list of charges against O'Rourke.

The principal charge was that he had protected and aided the escape of about eighty shipwrecked survivors of the Spanish Armada and received a letter of thanks from the King of Spain. Another charge, called lese-majeste, was that of insulting the Queen, 'that he caused her Majesty's name to be set on an image of a woman which he caused to be tied to a horse's tail and to be drawn through the mire'. Other charges related to his attacks on the counties Sligo and Roscommon. He was also accused of plotting to recruit mercenaries in Scotland to fight against the Queen in Ireland.

The trial of O'Rourke took place at a sitting of the court of Queen's Bench in Westminster Hall on 28 October 1591. As a prince descended from one of the ancient kings of Ireland, O'Rourke would not recognise the jurisdiction of the court. He would only submit to a trial by jury if he were allowed a good lawyer and if the Queen of England herself would sit as judge. These demands were refused and the trial proceeded.

Some five days later, O'Rourke was taken to the scaffold at Tyburn to

Tyburn, London.

suffer the wretched death of a traitor. He rejected the prayers of Miler
McGrath, the apostate Archbishop of Cashel, and berated him for his
betrayal saying, 'Do you remember the dignity from which you have
fallen? Return into the bosom of the ancient Church and learn from my
fortitude that lesson which you ought to have been the last on earth to
disavow.' O'Rourke's death was reported as follows:

> Upon Wednesdaie the 3 of November, Bren O'Royrke was drawn to
> Tyborne, and there hanged, his members and bowels burned in the fire,
> his heart taken out, and holden up by the hangman, naming it to be the
> archtraytor's heart, and then did he cast the same into the fire, then was his
> head stricken off, and his body quartered.

It really was the end; the eclipse of the power of the O'Rourkes of
Breifne. There would be other O'Rourkes to continue the fight, but
the image of the Gaelic chieftain standing firm against English laws had
gone forever.

Brian Oge O'Rourke
(Brian of the Battleaxes)
1584–1604

In the old Gaelic system of inheritance, leaders emerged from the extended family and the rights of sons born in or out of marriage was not a cause for argument. This system still persisted in the mindset of the Gaelic Lords of the sixteenth century. Perhaps it was one of the reasons, among many others, why Brian of the Ramparts fought so fiercely against the advance of English law into his territory. He saw his elder son Brian Oge as his successor but Brian Oge's mother was the wife of a Sligo merchant. Brian Oge's younger brother Hugh was son to his wife Lady Mary Burke, sister of the Earl of Clanricarde. This question of legitimacy would be of significance in later years.

As a young boy, Brian Oge was sent with his cousins, Clanricarde's sons, to be educated in Oxford. This practice had been adopted by the English in the hope of anglicising the sons of the chieftains and also as a guarantee of good behaviour by their fathers. The Lord Deputy, Sir John Perrot, recommended them to the Queen:

> They are pretty quick boys and would with good education I hope be good members of Christ and the commonwealth, and I therefore humbly pray you to procure that some good care be taken of them and their parents will bear most of the charge.

New College, Oxford.

While the Earl of Clanricarde went along with this plan for the education of his sons, it is clear that it was against the wishes of his brother-in-law, Brian of the Ramparts. He refused to pay for the upkeep of his son Brian Oge at Oxford. Four years later, in 1588, he arranged Brian Oge's escape from Oxford. Brian Oge enthusiastically helped his father in his final campaigns resisting English incursions into O'Rourke's country, earning his name to distinguish him from his father – Brian of the Battleaxes.

When Brian of the Ramparts made his fateful journey to Scotland, Brian Oge remained in Fermanagh. Following the shock news of his father's execution at Tyburn in 1591, he hoped to succeed to the lands and title in Breifne. He faced a huge task as he hovered on the borders of his territories with a small band of followers, making frequent raids into Connaught. In one raid, he carried off 400 cows from the old O'Rourke territory of Muintir Eolais, incurring the wrath of Sir Richard Bingham, Governor of Connaught, who made regular complaints about Brian's plundering activities. He referred to him as 'that young traitor O'Rourke', remarking that 'there were no rebels out against her Majesty except eighty beggarly traitors that follow O'Rourke and take refuge outside Connaught'.

In 1592, there was a brief cessation in his guerrilla warfare when Brian Oge, keen to get possession of his father's lands, submitted to the Queen, promising 'to live a true subject of my prince' and 'for anything I done amiss I cry her Majesties mercy and pardon'. His submission was rejected. Thereafter, in view of his lack of military strength, his only hope lay in forming alliances with other rebels such as the Maguires of Fermanagh, Red Hugh O'Donnell of Donegal, and Hugh O'Neill, Earl of Tyrone. The Maguires had sought to stop sheriffs introducing English laws into their territories by paying 400 cows to the Crown. This attempt at conciliation had failed, so the Maguires remained in rebellion.

Red Hugh O'Donnell had been imprisoned as a youth in Dublin Castle and had famously made his escape by sliding down a rope ladder, making his way with a companion through deep snows to Wicklow. His companion died from exposure. Now, he ruled in Tirconnell (Donegal), ready to resist any attempts to restrain his powers.

Hugh O'Neill was another of those boys sent to England to be educated. His sojourn there was longer than that of Brian Oge. He was just nine years old when Sir Henry Sidney took him into his home in Kent; he returned fifteen years later and in 1587 was made Earl of Tyrone. He was a loyal subject of the Queen for many years helping to put down Irish rebels in Munster. But in Ulster he ruled like a Gaelic chieftain, and when it was threatened by English bureaucracy, he resolved to fight against any reduction of his powers. He was in a strong position in the military sense, having by 1592 an army of 2,398 horse soldiers and 15,130 foot soldiers, plus a reserve of Scottish Gallowglasses.

It was fitting that Brian Oge would feel an affinity with Ulster; Leitrim was a passage to the North and featured the same inaccessibility of mountain, woods and bog. Ulster was now the last bastion of Gaelic

Hugh O'Neill.

Ireland. Besides, in 1585, when Connaught had accepted the agreement called the Composition of Connaught, whereby Irish chieftains became earls and agreed to pay a Composition rent, O'Rourke had refused to pay. This refusal resulted in Bingham entering Breifne and carrying off O'Rourke's cows. Of course O'Rourke retaliated by attacking Bingham at Ballymote, ravaging Ballymote and the surrounding countryside. Like Ulster he was determined to resist.

★ ★ ★ ★ ★

O'Neill and O'Donnell became the leaders of the rebellion in Ulster, which raged from 1592 to 1601 and was known as The Nine Years' War.

Brian Oge, always to the fore in the fighting, was present at the major events of that war. By 1594, O'Donnell had made several forays into Connaught accompanied by O'Rourke. O'Neill used scorched-earth methods as he advanced southwards towards the Pale. An English force was defeated at the Battle of the Ford of the Biscuits. The English leader, Sir Henry Bagenal, found it difficult to deal with the lightning ambushes of the rebels who then retreated into the woods. Queen Elizabeth was loath to release funds for an effective offensive against the rebels and by 1595 Sir John Norris was forced to a truce. O'Neill sought favourable terms for himself and O'Donnell and also for Maguire and O'Rourke. The Privy Council was adamant that while they would negotiate with O'Neill and O'Donnell that no such privilege be granted to either Maguire or O'Rourke. The truce continued into the following year.

In May 1596, Philip II of Spain, conscious of the shelter afforded to the survivors of the Spanish Armada by the O'Rourkes and Ulster, as well as the fact that he viewed their rebellion as a religious war against the Protestant Queen Elizabeth, sent a Spanish ship under Captain Alonso Cabos, which landed at Killybegs in May 1596. He bore letters for the northern chiefs with promises of help. Part of the King's letter to O'Rourke reads as follows:

> Seeing it is so noble a work to fight for the Catholic Faith when the enemies thereof endeavour so mightily to trample the same underfoot, I may not doubt that you who hitherto (as we hear) in the defense of God's cause have laboured so well, will now with might and main give yourself to the same cause.

O'Rourke's reply, dated 26 May 1596 says:

> I conceive that I have received an adequate reward for all toils and for the hardships I have endured from the tyrannical cruelty of the heretics, and that I am abundantly consoled when I call to mind the great generosity of your Majesty, expressed so fondly and lovingly in your letter.

Later that year, there was a surprise move against Brian Oge by his younger half-brother Teige. It was instigated by Sir John Norris who saw both the advantage of a feud and the attraction of a son related to the loyal Earl of Clanricarde. He wrote in a letter:

> We employed instruments into O'Rourke's country to draw a division between O'Rourke and his brother, for Teige O'Rourke being legitimate son of the late O'Rourke executed in England, by the sister of the Earl of Clanricarde, is of late entered into open faction against the other who is but the base brother, by which occasion the followers of the country are divided ... Teige was eager to oblige and was soon protesting loyalty: If I may have that which I ought to have under the Council's land, I protest to God and I pray the Lord that I may never enter the Kingdom of Heaven if I do not spend my blood, flesh and all that I can get in the world to do Her Majesties' service.

For Brian Oge, Teige's intervention was just another factor in his struggle; when he wasn't engaged in actual fighting, he was in a war of wits alternating between outright rebellion and possible submission. Judging which way his best advantage lay was difficult.

When the new Governor of Connaught, Sir Conyers Clifford, resolved to take Ballyshannon in order to cut off O'Donnell's access to the province, Brian Oge raced to join forces with O'Donnell. They succeeded in repulsing Clifford's efforts and engaged him in a running battle as far as Drumcliffe. But Sir Conyers Clifford was a clever man and brilliant in conciliatory efforts to achieve submission from the Irish chieftains. In his own words he saw the Irish as 'fickle, inconstant people and of necessity sometimes to be humoured according to their own natures'. In a matter of months he could say that all Connaught was pacified except for Brian O'Rourke. He confided in a letter that he would win over O'Rourke by a plot or else get his head. Clifford was dismissive of the claims of Teige O'Rourke saying, 'That man could not bring in a single man of the province or pay a penny of the Composition rent.'

In the face of the widespread submissions all around him in Connaught, the removal of the threat of his brother's claim, and the fact that the war had halted in another of the truces that punctuated the Nine Years' War, Brian Oge offered to submit, 'if he have his father's lands and at the same rent'. Clifford was keen to agree, remarking in derogatory fashion of the lands, 'which above all the counties in Ireland are of least value'. The Queen, anxious as always to avoid the horrendous cost of war, wrote to Clifford, 'We do hereby give you full authority (taking with you some such of our council as are in that province) and conclude with him [O'Rourke] and then for our best advantage and the resettling of that country in quietness and to assure him his lands.'

It is interesting that the English administration, in the tough realities of the situation, were prepared to overlook the matter of legitimacy. Brian Oge drew up a long list of demands, among them were the following:

> That he may receive under Her Majesties' most gracious pardon, with all his followers forgiveness of all the hurts they have done during the rebellion. That he may have his country both spiritual and temporal granted to him by patent. For the better defence of the county of Leitrim that a garrison be placed at Cavan and Ballymote and the garrisons answer to O'Rourke as often as he needs them. That he have a warrant not to be arrested without special direction of Her Majesty – asks this on account of what happened to his father.

In return, he promised to receive sheriffs into his territory, to be obedient to the services of the Queen and to pay the Composition rent. The settlement was made during the winter truce of 1597/8. But it was all too good to be true.

As June approached, signalling the end of the truce, Brian Oge sensed the tremendous energy emanating from O'Neill with his huge army and an impatient O'Donnell waiting to sweep into battle. Besides, he had learned that Ormonde was supporting Teige; he feared that Clifford was too weak to successfully defend his claims. Clifford was furious with Ormonde, saying that Teige O'Rourke 'was no instrument to be gained for Her Majesty'. Around this time, Brian Oge married Mary, daughter of Cuchonnacht Maguire and his wife Nuala, and sister of Sir Hugh Maguire.

Brian Oge's instincts proved correct; O'Neill headed for the Pale rousing rebellion there, and going on to victory in the great Battle of the Yellow Ford against Sir Henry Bagenal. O'Donnell advanced into Connaught, taking control, while in Munster a new Earl of Desmond was set up. Brian Oge joined with his old allies. He invaded Westmeath, killing 'some persons at Tyrell's Pass and returned home to his own country without wound or hurt'. His big moment of the war was to come at the Battle of the Curlew Mountains when, ironically, he would come face to face with Sir Conyers Clifford, the man who had so desperately sought to settle the problem of O'Rourke in a peaceful manner.

When O'Donnell attacked Sir Donough O'Connor of Sligo at Collooney, the new deputy, the Earl of Essex, favourite of Queen Elizabeth, ordered Clifford to go to O'Connor's aid. Clifford gathered a large army of both foot and horse soldiers in Roscommon and was joined by the sons of the Earl of Clanricarde and other Irish Earls, among them the O'Connor Don. They set out for Collooney and on 15 August they reached the foot of the Curlew Mountains. O'Donnell

Curlew Mountains. (*Photograph: Tommy Weir*)

had been aware of their advance and had prepared by felling trees to block the paths across the mountain and to afford cover for his men. He had chosen a spot at Bellaghboy to make his stand. However, it was a day of heavy rain and extremely dark skies. Nobody, least of all O'Donnell, thought that Clifford would undertake the treacherous terrain of rock, mud and bog in such conditions. But while O'Donnell remained in camp, Clifford, despite the exhaustion of his soldiers, gambled on this very assumption and forged ahead, leaving only the horse and baggage at a pass between Boyle and Ballinafad. He was surprised to find his way barred by Brian O'Rourke with 400 men. At the first volley of gunfire from Clifford, O'Rourke's troops ran for cover in the woods. From there, they persistently launched lightning attacks and ambushes on Clifford's soldiers as they tried desperately to cross the Curlew Mountains. Clifford's army were demoralised when one of their officers was killed. When Clifford was wounded many of the soldiers fled back to Boyle. O'Rourke ordered the decapitation of Clifford and sent his head to O'Donnell at Collooney. Despite this gruesome end, Clifford was given a respectful burial in the monastery of Loch Ce. There is evidence of regret at his death by some of the Irish for 'he never told them a lie and was a bestower of gifts and treasures'.

By 1600, all Ireland (save for a small area around Dublin) was under the control of the rebels. The Earl of Essex had left Ireland in disgrace to explain his failure in crushing the rebellion to an angry Queen Elizabeth, but by February, she had dispatched two more formidable men to Ireland; Lord Mountjoy as the new Lord Deputy and Sir George Carew as President of Munster. Carew had some almost immediate success in quietening Munster. While Mountjoy kept O'Neill busy in Munster, one of his officers set up a garrison at Derry. This was a major inroad to the North and a blow to O'Donnell's former strong position. Nevertheless, the rebels, especially O'Neill, still remained a serious threat.

There was some dissension in their ranks with personal feuds. Brian Oge O'Rourke must have felt great consternation when his half-brother Teige married Hugh O'Donnell's sister. For a while it cooled his relationship with O'Donnell. It had long been a policy with the English to divide and conquer and they were quick to seize this opportunity. There was a plot to murder O'Donnell, Teige O'Rourke, and O'Connor Sligo and it was suggested in a letter that Brian O'Rourke 'might easily be drawn to join … in this service because I know he would be glad to settle his estate and would be quieter if Teige be killed with O'Donnell'. The plan fell through and there is no evidence that Brian ever knew of it. But Teige's profile had been raised and O'Donnell sent him into Munster to aid the rebellion there. Brian was forced into a working relationship with his brother.

Gradually support for O'Donnell was undermined in the North when his brother-in-law Niall Garve O'Donnell and the O'Dohertys submitted to the English. Similarly, in Munster Carew gained ground and was able to send 1,000 men to Boyle to 'keep O'Rourke at bay and curb O'Donnell'. O'Neill was under heavy pressure from Mountjoy, who campaigned right through the winter. But matters took a dramatic turn when, in September 1601, Don Juan Del Aquila arrived in Kinsale with an army of Spanish soldiers to help the rebels. This was the moment the rebels had long awaited.

At Ballymote there was a great gathering of forces including O'Donnell, Brian Oge O'Rourke, O'Connor Roe, Mc Dermot of

Ballymote Castle. (*Photograph: Tommy Weir*)

Moylurg, and some of the Burkesa; it was a combined force of 3,000 men and 400 horsemen. They set out on the long trek to Kinsale. O'Neill advanced from Leinster. Morale was high and the combined Irish armies numbered some 12,000. But crucially, the Battle of Kinsale proved an utter disaster for the Irish. Against all the odds it was a victory for a possibly astonished English force when the Irish were routed before the Spanish had even entered the fray. The Battle of Kinsale in 1601 was a collapse of major proportions in the struggle against Tudor domination in Ireland. The die was cast for the humiliating submission of O'Neill at Mellifont two years later. Queen Elizabeth, at last awake to the danger from Ireland, had by this time dispatched 20,000 soldiers to the country. In the disarray following the battle the Irish chieftains fled. O'Donnell fled to Spain where he died a year later and was believed to have been poisoned.

After Kinsale, Brian O'Rourke rushed home to Breifne on hearing that his brother Teige had availed of his absence to assume the chieftaincy. He positioned himself at Leitrim Castle, the last castle built by the O'Rourkes, while Teige was in possession of the castle in Dromahaire. A few months later, he joined forces with Rory O'Donnell and O'Connor Sligo, in an effort to stop the advance of the new Governor of Connaught Sir Oliver Lambert into Sligo, but to no avail.

Donal Cam O'Suilleabhain Beare, of the Beare peninsula in Kerry, was another Irish Lord who had joined forces with O'Neill and O'Donnell at the Battle of Kinsale. After the battle he remained in rebellion, but in 1602 Sir George Carew mounted a fierce siege on his castle at Dunboy. The castle was taken and all the defenders killed and executed. Donal Cam, realising the hopelessness of his situation and knowing that Brian Oge was still holding out in Breifne, decided to seek protection there and also make contact with the northern chiefs. Thus began one of the most famous marches in Irish history. On 31 December 1602, he set off with some 1,000 of his followers, of which about half were soldiers and among them women and children, on a journey of 200 miles.

The march was truly heroic and beset with all manner of hardship. They were under constant attack from both the English and native Irish. There were several skirmishes and battles with the English as they moved northwards. Hunger drove them to raid houses, taking sacks of wheat and barley and whatever food they could find, thus alienating some of the Irish. Many were killed or left behind in a weakened state.

Donal Cam
O'Suilleabhain Beare.
(*Courtesy of Maynooth
College*)

It was winter and the terrain was stony, boggy, muddy and icy. It was bitterly cold but when they lit fires to warm themselves, they signalled their
presence to the English, who attacked and so their numbers diminished
steadily. Later accounts testify to their desperation and will to overcome
obstacles. On one occasion, they reached the Shannon only to find that
all boats had been removed to prevent their crossing. According to an
account later written by O'Suilleabhain's nephew Philip, 'the soldiers
were nerveless from want and every heart was filled with giant despair'.

O'Sullivan Beare organised the building of two ships by felling some trees and killing twelve horses. The account of the building of the ships was as follows:

Two rows of osiers were planted opposite each other, the thickest end being stuck in the ground, and the other ends bent in to meet each other's vis-à-vis, to which they were fastened with cords, and so formed the frame of the ship turned upside down. To this frame the solid planks were fixed, and seats and cross beams were fitted inside. Outside it was covered with the skins of eleven horses, and oars and dowels were fitted on. The keel was flat, both on account of the material used and in order to avoid rocks and stones. It was twenty-six feet long, six feet broad and five feet deep, but the prow was a little higher in order to stem the tide.

Another smaller boat was built and covered with the skin of a horse. With these two boats O'Sullivan managed to ferry most of his people over the river, drawing after them the horses which swam across. But not all made it; they were under attack almost immediately and in the ensuing fight, some of the followers were killed while others fled in panic.

They passed many places on that long journey: Ballyvourney; Pobble O'Keeffe, near Millstreet; Ardpatrick in Limerick; Solloghead; Ballinakill; Latteragh in Tipperary; Aughrim in Galway, and Ballinlough, Roscommon, before they reached the woods close to Boyle in Co. Sligo. Here they rested and a guide appeared who offered to lead them to O'Rourke's castle in Leitrim where they were assured of a warm welcome. The appearance of this guide must have been viewed as miraculous, for in an early account he was a white-clothed figure wearing a wreath and carrying a wand. O'Sullivan's account states:

There stood the battlements of the castle of Dromahaire, which was O'Rourke's chief place, these many centuries, since Tiernan O'Rourke lorded it over Breffni long ago. There too at Dromahaire stood the most beautiful friary of the northern county: the famous abbey of Creevelea, within whose walls the Prince of Breffni was buried in his chiselled tomb, and on the cloisters are carved trees and birds and St Francis preaching. Ah, but that princely place is not the present abode of an O'Rourke worthy

Creevelea Abbey, Dromahaire. (*Photograph: Grace Weir*)

Cloisters, Creevelea Abbey, detail. (*Photograph: Grace Weir*)

of the name. A little while since, Bingham of Connaught, Lambert's predecessor, rode into Dromahaire, stabled his horses in Creevelea's walls, burnt its rare wood-work for his troopers' cooking fires, and ended the sway of the princes of Breffni and the masses and psalms of the friars in their protection. After Kinsale, a Queen's O'Rourke was put into the castle Tadhg (Teige) by name: and there he sits to-day, O'Sullivan, no friend to you! No, but the true O'Rourke, Brian Og by name, he who was with you and O'Neill at that dread battle, he still holds the south of Breffni. He has a stronghold, Leitrim Fort. It lies yonder, a dozen miles distant … that is your goal.

The last stage of the journey proved difficult. The ghastly effects of the long march are recalled in the description of the feet of one of the group, a man called O'Connor. O'Sullivan tells us:

The greater part of his feet and legs was inflamed. Lividness supervened, and in turn gave place to blisters, and these were succeeded by ulcers. He was terribly afflicted and only able to bear up because he suffered for Christ Jesus. In the dead of night they reached the little village called Knockvicar, where they refreshed themselves with fire and purchased food. When they decided to move on, O'Connor, whose ulcers had been crustated by the fire, was not able to stand, much less walk. Four of his comrades carried him on their shoulders until in the twilight they found a stray beast, lank and worn with age, on which they placed him without bridle or saddle, the sharp bone of the lean back pricking the rider. Some led the blind beast, others whacked him along. They crossed the Curlews and slowly made their way to the sanctuary of O'Rourke's castle.

A thousand people had set out two weeks earlier from Glengariff, now only thirty-five remained. Amongst the soldiers and followers there was one woman. In a manner reminiscent of his father, who had welcomed the survivors of the Spanish Armada, Brian Oge extended hospitality to these survivors of an epic march, a journey of over 200 miles. He gave directions for the care of the sick. In the village of Leitrim a plaque on the only part that remains of Leitrim Castle commemorates their achievement. As soon as he had rested, Donal Cam lost no time in going further north to Fermanagh to join with the Maguires still in rebellion. But with the news of O'Neill's surrender to Mountjoy in 1603, he took

Leitrim Castle. (*Photograph: Joe Walker*)

ship to Spain, where he was welcomed by King Philip III. A few years later he was assassinated.

★ ★ ★ ★ ★

In 1603, following the death of Queen Elizabeth, James I was crowned King of England. One of his first acts was to offer pardon to all the Irish chieftains involved in the recent rebellion, on condition they submit and promise loyalty to the Crown. Most of the chieftains availed of this and soon Mountjoy was accepting submissions, including a very humble one from the once proud O'Neill, Earl of Tyrone, who made his submission on his knees and in tears. Mountjoy could report to the King in January 1603 that all chieftains of Connaught had submitted except for one, 'only the proud and faithless Brian O'Rourke nothwithstanding his former humble submission to the Lord Deputy to be received to mercy, absented himself'. But Brian O'Rourke was in a difficult position, he knew that even if he did submit the English would support the claims of his brother Teige above his own, that they saw Teige as the legitimate heir. It was a dilemma. So he remained in rebellion, no doubt in desperation about his future prospects.

Mountjoy made careful plans for a final onslaught on O'Rourke. He planned a three-pronged attack from south Connaught, Sligo and Longford under the overall command of Sir Oliver Lambert, Governor of Connaught. In March 1603, a force of 3,000 men was at the banks of the Shannon opposite Leitrim Castle. Brian O'Rourke, defending strongly, successfully thwarted all their efforts to cross the river. The siege lasted for twelve days until one English officer, John Bostock, managed to ferry some soldiers across in pontoons possibly under the cover of darkness. He stationed themselves in a chapel and from there, carried out raids on O'Rourke's country laying it waste and carrying off cattle. O'Rourke retaliated and in a running battle defeated Bostock. But a major blow was dealt to O'Rourke when his brother Teige arrived to attack him in his castle and, more importantly, managed to convince many of Brian's followers to throw their lot in with him. He was also under siege by Rory O'Donnell who was angry with him for his refusal to allow O'Donnell the use of his castle after the defeat at Kinsale.

A month later, Brian O'Rourke wrote to Mountjoy reminding him of his earlier offers of submission and the difficulties which forced him to continue 'this loathsome life'. He asked to be received by Mountjoy. But Mountjoy was giving full support to Teige and reported in a letter to England:

In Connaught all is quiet except O'Rourke's country who is already reduced to fly as a wood-kerne from place to place with not above three score men. His brother the legitimate son of the old O'Rourke (for this man is a bastard) is now with him in Dublin. He has already prosecuted his brother and is more mighty for them and with a little help will be able utterly to banish him. So that although O'Rourke sueth for mercy he thinks it no policy to receive him for his brother that has more rights would be able to do harm if he were not contented and it is it for sons of that blood to have that whom the people will obey; and it is good for no man else for none but devils would dwell in such a hell. He has only promised Teige O'Rourke to be a means to the King to bestow the country upon him reserving what shall be thought just.

It is clear from the letter that English policy dictated that they would deal only with the man who held power. The matter of Brian Oge's legitimacy was not an issue at an earlier stage when Teige posed no threat. His use of the word 'hell' to describe O'Rourke's country gives some idea of the anarchy reigning at this time. Brian Oge made one last effort and wrote directly to King James:

> In the reign of Elizabeth late Queen of England my father Bryan O'Rourke … was so cruelly used by divers of Her Majesty's officers as he was forced to abandon his country and for the safety of his life to run to Scotland where he was not suffered to repair before your Majesty but was committed and sent into England, where remaining some while prisoner in the Tower of London was at length put to death, through which and for that the pretence then was to seize upon all his lands and country; he was forced in defence to enter into acts of war against them and so ever sithence to have continued much against his will, until that God Almighty did now cast upon your Majesty James the dominion the said Queen possessed … Wherefore he most humbly beseeches Your Majesty to vouchsafe unto him a taste of His Majesty's most gracious favour in admitting him to enjoy his said father's inheritance and His Majesty's most gracious secure pass to repair into his presence thereby to make his estate further known.
>
> *May 4 1603, Leitrim.*

One is forced to wonder what Brian Oge thought of his chances but clearly he felt he could make a better case in a person to person audience with the King; he also shows his nervousness in asking for a pass to guarantee his safety. But James I was having none of it and a few months later he wrote to the Earl of Devonshire, Lord Lieutenant of Ireland. The letter dated 11 September 1603 states:

> King's letter in favour of Teige O'Rowrke, the only legitimate son of Sir Bryan O'Rowrke, lately executed for treason, whereas by the attainder of Sir Bryan O'Rowrke, Knight, lately executed for high treason within this kingdom, the county or lordship of Brenny Jrowrke and Moynterolis otherwise called O'Rourke's country in the county of Leitrim with such lands in the counties adjoining as ever the rightful inheritance and free-

hold of the said Sir Bryan, came to the lands of the king's dear sister Elizabeth and so descended to the king himself … manifold services of the said Teige O'Rourke done lately within this kingdom worthy of recompense and his forwardness to continue his dutiful loyalty, the king thought good of his free gift to grant unto him and his heirs male of his body all and singular, the countries and lordships with all manors, castles which rightfully belonged to his said father.

To make matters worse, Rory O'Donnell chose this moment to plunder Breifne and seize Dromahaire. This was in retaliation for Brian Oge's refusal to give him support after Kinsale, and also, of course, O'Donnell's sister was married to Teige. An added attraction was the fact that Mountjoy gave him the understanding that he would receive some of O'Rourke's lands. Brian Oge fled to a Franciscan monastery at Ross-Iriala in Galway. According to O'Sullivan Beare he died of a fever, 'deserted by those to whom he had entrusted his government', in January 1604. But a suspicion remains that he was poisoned by Lambert. He was aged thirty-five. The *Annals of the Four Masters* pay tribute to him as follows:

> He was the supporting pillar and battle prop of Ardh-Finn, the tower of battle for prowess, the star of valour and rivalry of the High-Briúin, a brave protecting man who had not suffered Breifne to be molested in his time, a sedate and heroic man, kind to friends, fierce to foes; and the most illustrious that had come for some time of his family for clemency, hospitality, nobleness, firmness and steadiness.

In 1605 the Lord Lieutenant, Earl of Devonshire, gave warning that Teige O'Rourke was seriously ill and was already speculating about the future of his lands at Breifne, 'There is a likelihood of the death of O'Rourke, whose country if he die will be wholly at the King's disposition for it was to him and his heirs male and heirs he hath none.' When Teige died shortly afterwards at the early age of twenty-eight, the *Annals of the Four Masters* paid him tribute:

> O'Rourke (Teige, son of Brian, son of Owen) Lord of Breifne, a man who had experienced many hardships and difficulties while defending his patrimony against his brother Brian Og, a man who was not expected to die in his bed, but by the spear or sword, a man who had fought many

difficult battles while struggling for his patrimony and the dignity of his father, until God at length permitted him to obtain the lordship, died and was interred with due honours in the Franciscan Friary of Carrickpatrick (Creevelea Abbey).

Teige had two sons, Brian and Hugh. They were born while their mother Mary O'Donnell was still married to Donal O'Cahan. Brehon law allowed for this but there was an ominous ring to the Lord Lieutenant's words, 'heirs he hath none'. It did not bode well for his elder son Brian, aged six at the time of his father's death.

The Villiers Connection

The ruins of Villiers Castle dominate the approach into the village of Dromahaire. Seven tall chimneys tower upwards over the remains of a stone building. Nearby, closer to the River Bonet, lie the ruins of O'Rourke's banqueting hall, its stone strangulated by tough ivy. The latter is in a very fragmented state, as the stones from this castle were taken and used in the construction of Villiers Castle. Both ruins encapsulate the story of Ireland's past – the Irish Chieftain replaced by the English Planter.

George Villiers, Duke of Buckingham, favourite of King James I of England and recipient of the O'Rourke lands, in fact never lived in this castle for he was assassinated before it was even built. His acquisition of the O'Rourke territory is a bizarre tale of ambition and greed on his part but it was facilitated by King James's complete infatuation with him. However amazing his story, it is overshadowed by the extremely tragic tale of Brian O'Rourke, son of Sir Teige O'Rourke, nephew of Brian Oge O'Rourke and last heir to the O'Rourke lands. They met only once, when Brian O'Rourke was twenty-two and George Villiers was thirty, but their lives were closely linked.

The Plantation of Leitrim was first mooted in a report sent to King James in 1608, six years before George Villiers's arrival at Court. In the famous Flight of the Earls a year earlier, the Earls of Tyrone and Tyreconnell with their families and allies, had sailed from Lough

Villiers Castle, Dromahaire. (*Photograph:Tommy Weir*)

Swilly to the continent following the failure of the Nine Years' War. They were proclaimed traitors and their lands were forfeited to the Crown. A survey and a projected plan for the Plantation of Ulster swiftly followed, comprising the counties Tyrone, Donegal, Fermanagh, Armagh, Coleraine and Cavan. By 1609, some 500,000 acres had been thrown open to settlers. At the same time a report was sent to King James urging that Leitrim should also be planted.

The suggestion that Leitrim should be included was, at the very least, surprising. Until this time, only the lands of rebellious chieftains who refused to submit to the Crown were considered fair game for plantation. It was the King himself, only four years previously, who had granted the Lordship of West Breifne including the demesne of Dromahaire to Brian's father Sir Teige. Teige O'Rourke, who had been considered by the English to be the lawful heir to the O'Rourke lands instead of his rebellious brother Brian Oge, died at the early age of twenty-eight in 1606. Brian Oge had died two years earlier aged thirty-five. Later the question was at least asked – had they been poisoned?

Sir Teige left two young sons, Brian and Hugh. Brian, aged six, was the elder brother and as the future heir was made a royal ward and placed in the care of the Earl of Clanricarde, who was a loyal subject of the King. When Brian was twelve he was sent to Trinity College where he remained for four years. From there, he went to New College, Oxford, the same college from which his uncle Brian Oge had escaped. Several relations of the Earl of Clanricarde had also attended Oxford, presumably for grooming as civilized subjects of the King. Of Brian, it was reported that he was 'carefully bred in a degree suitable to his estate and quality'. From Oxford he was admitted to the Middle Temple of the Inns of Court in London. There was the expectation that when he would come of age he would take over in Breifne as a loyal subject of the King. But obviously from as early as 1608, when the report was written, there was a determination to prevent him from inheriting. Apart

King James I.

from a deep distrust of the O'Rourkes, the lure of plantation was proving to be a strong incentive.

The report sent to King James was written in neat rounded handwriting by an unknown writer. It makes a compelling case for the 'absolute necessity of a British plantation in the County of Leitrim commonly called O'Rourke's country'. Describing the natives as 'ever being the first out in action and last in submission to the Crown', he points out that the area is the only passage of danger between the provinces of Connaught and Leinster adding that 'the security of the Ulster Plantation doth much depend upon the provident Plantation of the said Rourke's country'. He states that the physical nature of the place, which 'being full of bogs, woods, mountains, glens – wild and unhaunted wasteness hath never been other than an inaccessible den and nursery of thieves and doth easily invite evil disposed minds to wicked designs'.

In the absence of a rebellion, whereby O'Rourke could be proclaimed a traitor and his lands forfeited, another excuse for plantation would have to be found. O'Rourke's title to the lands must be revealed to be faulty. The report does this to devastating effect. O'Rourke, he states, 'is openly known to be a bastard and as such has little right to claim over and above the 80 quarters of land granted to his grandfather Sir Brian O'Rourke'. The charge of 'bastard' was later confirmed by a jury who found Brian O'Rourke and his brother to be bastards, 'by reason their mother was first married to an Irish lord in the north, from whom she was divorced by the Roman Catholic clergy, which not been consistent with the laws of England, the sons were declared illegitimate'.

An early case, perhaps, of Church annulment versus legal divorce. The report warns against the delaying of the plantation, 'until the Ward come to years for since it is true that the boy is a bastard, he being in likelihood to prove an unhappy youth, the longer the detecting thereof be deferred is the longer to keep your Majesty from your right and the country from good'.

In a nod to the possible rights of young O'Rourke he says, 'and if your Majesty should be graciously pleased to favour the boy with some land there, 20 quarters in a civil plantation will be more beneficial to him than all the country in that barbarous estate as hitherto the O'Rourkes have kept the same'. He goes on that, 'the plantation would be with men, honest, industrious and of good temper, men of quality and able undertaking, neither the barbarism of the inhabitants nor the thievishness of the country will corrupt them. For it is good people that maketh a good country.'

No doubt James read the report with great interest. From the start of his reign he was committed to the idea of plantation. It would serve many purposes. Firstly, it would keep an unruly people in order, exactly in line with the sentiments expressed in the report. Secondly, he was short of money. In contrast to the careful, tightfisted handling of finance by Queen Elizabeth, James was wildly extravagant, showering rewards on his Scottish friends, staging highly expensive masquerades and plays for entertainment, and giving lavish banquets. There is a record of one banquet that cost more than £3,000, needing 100 cooks for eight days, to produce 1,600 dishes which included 240 pheasants. The mechanical devices, used in the masques devised by Ben Johnson and Inigo Jones, cost at one stage, £1,400 a year. Small wonder that the royal coffers were in a perilous state. The Ulster Plantation would serve to pay for the high cost of the Nine Years' War, soldiers being granted lands instead of money for their services. Thirdly, there was the glory aspect. James had been King of Scotland and was now King of England. The idea of a Kingdom of England, Scotland and Ireland was attractive; the dream of a Great Britain was emerging.

Brian O'Rourke continued his studies unaware of any plans to deprive him of his inheritance. He was fourteen years old when a young man of twenty-two arrived at the court of King James: one George Villiers.

George Villiers was the son of a small Leicestershire landowner. Brought up by his widowed mother he learned music, dancing and fencing, and at the age of sixteen went to France for three years. There he acquired all the skills of a courtier. He was also astonishingly good-looking. Even the soberest of people bear testimony to this fact. 'He was one of the handsomest men in the whole world', wrote Sir John Oglander. Two bishops competed for the most laudatory description. 'From the nails of his fingers – nay from the site of his foot to the crown of his head, there was no blemish in him. The setting of his looks, every motion, every bending of his body was admirable', wrote Bishop Harket. Bishop Goodman expanded:

All that sat in the Council looking steadfastly on him, saw his face as if it had been the face of an angel. He was the handsomest-bodied man in England and of so sweet a disposition – I have heard it from two men and very great men that he was as inwardly beautiful as he was outwardly.

George Villiers by Renold Elstrack, 1571. (*Yale Center for British Art, Gift of George A. Douglass.*)

Sir Seymour D'Evans, 'saw everything in him full of delicacy and hand-some features'.

Villiers was introduced at Court in 1614 and James was instantly smitten. He was made the King's Cup-Bearer; the word went out, 'a youth named Villiers begins to be in favour with his Majesty'. James's long-suffering wife Queen Anne, having endured 'favourites both in England and Scotland was very shie to adventure upon another'. The situation was formalised in a ceremony in the Queen's bedchamber. The Queen called upon their son Prince Charles for his sword and presented it to the King who thereupon knighted Villiers and made him Gentleman of the Bedchamber. In this role as a kind of super-valet he was close to the King and all matters confidential. In 1616, he was appointed Master of the Horse despite his inexperience in the saddle. On August 9 the Court papers read, 'The King was yesterday feasted at dinner by Sir George Villiers mother' and two weeks later on August 23, 'On Tuesday Sir George Villiers shall have his creation of Viscount and Baron both together.' His meteoric rise continued, for in 1619 he was made First Minister; four years later he was created Earl and then Duke of Buckingham. The title of Duke was all the more remarkable, for he was the first Duke in a hundred years who was not of royal line-age. This elevation was rushed through in secret. Camden reports:

> The Lord Chancellor sent for me before seven in the morning and pri-vately charged me on the oath both of my allegiance as a subject and my oath as king of arms to keep secret that which he was to impart unto me, namely, that the King purposed to make the Earl of Buckingham Marquess of Buckingham without ceremony, only by delivering the patent before any of the Council knew it, which the King did in his wisdom to avoid counterposition and competition of others.

But indeed, the Privy Council and the entire Court were left in no doubt about the feelings of the King towards George Villiers, when James declared to an astonished court:

> You may be sure that I love the Earl of Buckingham more than anyone else and more than you who are here assembled. I wish to speak in my own behalf and not to have it thought a defect, for Jesus Christ did the same, and therefore I cannot be blamed – Christ had his John and I have my George.

George Villiers was in a position of enormous power and privilege. Those seeking favours from the King had first to negotiate with Villiers and frequently made payments of money to win his support. The Venetian Ambassador, writing about him in 1619 reports, 'The King's favour renders him the chief authority and the entire court obeys his will. All requests pass through his hands and without his favour it is difficult to obtain anything or reach the King's ear.' Inevitably, his friends and relations benefited; honours and titles were distributed freely but with cash payments to Villiers. Again the Venetian Ambassador remarked, no doubt ironically, 'The number of titled persons is so constantly multiplied that they are no longer distinguished from the common people.'

In Ireland, Sir Oliver St John, related by marriage to the Villiers family, was created Viscount Grandison of Limerick and later became Vice Admiral of Connaught. His nephew, George St John commanded the fort at Carrick-on-Shannon, while another nephew became Governor of Athlone. No wonder Sir Oliver paid open tribute to George Villiers as 'the only author of my fortunes'. Another of Villiers's beneficiaries was Sir Francis Aungier, who acquired interest in the royal castle and lands in Granard, Co. Roscommon, which included 3,000 acres of prime land and 1,298 acres of wood and bog. He was created Baron of Longford in 1621. While George himself received revenue from Ireland, such as custom fees and income for warrants which investigated land titles, he was still very much the landless younger son. His older brother William holding the family seat at Brokesby.

The fragility of his situation, resting as it was on the grace and favour of the King, was brought into sharp focus, when the King became gravely ill in April 1619, just a month after the death of the Queen. His future needed to be secured. He undoubtedly confided his fears to the King when he recovered from his illness, for James gave him his wholehearted support. When in the following year, George married Katherine Manners, daughter of the Earl of Rutland, James gave his blessing. Simon Schama remarks on James's lack of jealousy towards the heterosexual needs of his favourites. George now had an estate at Burley-on-the-Hill but it had cost £28,000. He was settled but without a fortune. Acquisition of lands in Ireland must suddenly have appeared as an attractive proposition.

Perhaps at the time it did not seem significant, but it was also in March 1619 when the King had fallen ill, that a portentous incident occurred. Brian O'Rourke, now aged twenty, celebrated St Patrick's Day with some of his Irish friends. Returning home after supper, in heightened good spirits, they met up with some others. A drunken brawl broke out and some were injured, one man suffering a 'broken pate'. Brian O'Rourke was arrested to Gatehouse Prison at Westminster Palace and ordered to be detained until he paid a fine of £300. Not an earth-shattering event, but one that would have tragic repercussions for young Brian O'Rourke. From early on, it appears evident that he was being detained for a period over and above what would have been expected. Again a question arises: was the fracas a set-up? Later that year, he trustfully sent the first of numerous petitions for release. It was addressed to the King himself. There is something oddly poignant about a young man writing in verse:

> O! in light thy hart with a sacred fier
> Glorious great King, grant but my desire
> O doe but grant that most gracious favour
> Now in my misery to prove my savior.
> Libertie sweet Sir is that I crave,
> O grant but that, and then my life you have.
> In the meantime I am bound to pray
> For thee my sovrayne long to bear sway
> And from your enemies may you always bee
> Garded by heaven's greatest polisie.

James must have been reminded of that other plea for help from his grandfather, that other Brian O'Rourke whom he had delivered to Queen Elizabeth for certain execution. In November, the Privy Council, possibly surprised at his lengthy incarceration, wrote to the Chief Justice to release Brian O'Rourke from the imprisonment he had so long endured. Ominously, nothing happened. It would take some years for it to become clear that from 1619 onwards, George Villiers was secretly nurturing ambitions for the acquisition of O'Rourke's territory in the likely event of a plantation.

However, the whole matter of plantation in Ireland was giving concern to the Privy Council. In 1615, an official survey of the Ulster Plantation found much to fault. Those who had received land were failing in their contract for the building and resettlement of their estates.

They had not succeeded in replacing the native Irish with British settlers, or so the report said. On the other hand, an obviously puzzled Lord Deputy was forced to admit that lands were so well replanted that 'not much room is left for the natives'. In January 1620, Sir Francis Bacon felt there was a need to study the 'better processing of the Plantation of Ireland'. In June Sir William Parsons went to London to report on the poor progress of plantation in Longford.

In July 1620, a meeting of the Privy Council took place, which could possibly impinge on the hopes of George Villiers. Sir Francis Blundell read letters from Ireland concerning plantations and mentioned the proposed Plantation of Leitrim. This, apparently, gave rise to a lively discussion about the defects of the plantations of Ulster, Wexford and Longford, 'for their lordships fell all upon a joint resolution to move his Majesty that the three former plantations might be exactly surveyed, reviewed and reformed before they should settle that of Leitrim'. This was bad news for an impatient and land-hungry Villiers.

A month after this meeting, James went to Hampton Court for the summer recess. While there, George Villiers availed of the opportunity to press and convince James to proceed with the Leitrim plantation. One problem was the absence of a submission and surrender of the lands by O'Rourke to the Crown. Brian O'Rourke had come of age and while the Crown had disputed his title, it would simplify matters if he would personally surrender the lands to the King. At this crucial moment Brian was betrayed by his guardian, the Earl of Clanricarde. Briefed that a plantation was being planned, Clanricarde passed over his wardship of Brian O'Rourke to the King, in return for anything he liked in Ireland, up to a value of £1,500. It was clearly a deal. There would be no one to defend young Brian O'Rourke in his claim to his father's lands. This support was sorely needed during that summer of 1620 when George Villiers took action to pursue the matter of plantation in Leitrim into his own hands.

No doubt Brian O'Rourke was surprised when one day he was suddenly marched from his prison cell, taken by coach under guard to Hampton Court and summoned into the presence of George Villiers, Duke of Buckingham. He was formally requested to submit his title, acknowledge the right of the King and acquiesce to the plantation. A shocked Brian O'Rourke refused to agree to any of these requests.

Tower of London. (*Photograph: Viki Male*)

George Villiers was flanked by members of the Privy Council but O'Rourke was not intimidated. In the battle of wills between the two young men O'Rourke remained adamant. He had by this time spent two years in prison but he showed the same pride as his grandfather Sir Bryan O'Rourke, who had been dubbed 'the proudest man in Ireland'. He probably also experienced the same sense of disbelief regarding the repercussions. Some twenty years later and still imprisoned, he recalled the event, that in 1620 he was 'sent for to Hampton Court to appear before the privy council and there, by the then Duke of Buckingham, required to submit to the Plantation of his estate, which he refusing to do, was then forthwith committed to the Gatehouse and thence to the Tower'. As a young man, with a sense of the injustice of his imprisonment, he could not have foreseen that as a result of his refusal he would remain a prisoner for the rest of his life.

It was obvious that James would be highly distrustful of the grandson of the man who had given help to the survivors of the Spanish Armada, of the nephew of the rebel, Brian Oge O'Rourke, who had fought in the Nine Years' War, distrustful also of his potential to stir trouble in Ireland. It was easy to forget his pledge of the lands to his father Teige for his support. It was fortunate indeed that Teige's heir was safely in prison. Besides, he wanted to indulge his favourite, his 'Steenie' – a pet name for Villiers, which apparently was an abbreviation of St Stephan who reputedly had the face of an angel.

Following the abortive encounter between Brian O'Rourke and George Villiers, the remainder of the summer recess was devoted to the drawing up of the instructions or detailed plan for the Plantation of Leitrim. This was done by Sir Francis Blundell, the Surveyor General, and was imparted to a full council assembly at Hampton Court by King James himself. Brian O'Rourke was formally dispossessed of his lands and kept out of Ireland, 'where he may be offensive to the Planters by means of such idle persons as may resort to him as followers or dependents of his supposed father, Sir Teige'.

There were some differences to previous plantations in this Plantation of Leitrim. It did not follow a rebellion as other plantations had, but signalled the start of a policy of continuous plantation. Like Longford, it was an extension of the Ulster Plantation, spreading southwards and westwards into the midlands. Another change was that half of O'Rourke's territory was to be assigned to newcomers, in contrast to the quarter in earlier plantations. Also, despite criticism of the difficulties involved in the management of excessively large estates, the recommendations of the council for smaller estates were ignored, 'We have thought fit to assign to some few men of special quality larger estates to provide support and encouragement against the barbarous Irish residing in those parts.' The King was overheard to remark that Buckingham was to have first choice. A later report bluntly stated, that 'order was given for this last plantation … against the opinion of most of the lords'. Their misgivings were assuaged by an assurance that planting would only follow the voluntary submission of the natives.

George Villiers was granted 6,500 acres of good land and 1,500 acres of bog in the heartland of O'Rourke's country at Dromahaire. Many of his relations and supporters also received lands, among them his brother Sir Edward Villiers and nephew Sir William Villiers. Others included Sir William Parsons, William Burke, and the surveyor, Sir Nicholas Pinnar. Sir Teige's widow was granted as a dower 1,600 acres of land and 3,411 of bog but only for the period of her lifetime. By 1622 there was a new Lord Deputy: Henry Viscount Falkland. He reported that the natives seemed glad to make their dependence on the Crown and to 'relinquish the old over-grown title of O'Rourke'. He would later seek estates for his two sons.

As the plantation proceeded, the plight of Brian O'Rourke became progressively more desperate. His appeals for help and release are heart-rending and his own words of 'pitiful' and 'miserable' best describe his situation. Though imprisoned, he was expected to pay for his keep. The pension which Brian O'Rourke was supposed to receive, £400 a year, had not been paid. In 1620, he petitioned the Privy Council:

> Most humbly sheweth that, that as your Lordships well knoweth, your suppliant's whole estate is detained in his Majesty's hands, since and during your petitioner's minority, he having as yet nothing left to live on but bare [illegible] for his allowance, during his wardship, whereof your suppliant not having received a penny for these four years past, he hath been forced to go naked, had he not asked some poor friend's credit for his poor clothes, which, resting unpaid, hath left both him and them utterly void of all further supply.

He goes on:

> ...to beseech your Lordships to mediate with my Lord Treasurer for the payment unto your suppliant of the said arrearages, and the preventing of any such future extremities as he hath now long suffered. It being a pitiful thing that a man whose whole estate is detained should thus miserably starve in prison, which your Lordships taking into your gracious consideration, he shall daily pray for your Lordships' present and eternal happiness.

His appeals for aid were obviously ignored, for by 1624 there is a record of some '12 letters and petitions by Brian O'Rourke to Cranfield [the Lord Treasurer], relating to his debts and the pension he is not receiving from the Exchequer (£240 outstanding). He is unable to pay off his debts until he receives the money.'

Some examples give a picture of the difficulties he endured in his imprisonment:

> 1622: Petition of the creditors of Brian O'Rourke. The King has his estate, and he cannot pay a penny.
>
> 1623: Petition of Isabell Gettrey to Cranfield to pay a provisions' debt owed by Brian O'Rourke, prisoner in the Gatehouse.
>
> 1623: Petition of Anne, widow of Francis Nash. She has supplied 72 pounds on bond to Brian O'Rourke, Co. Leitrim for his maintenance.

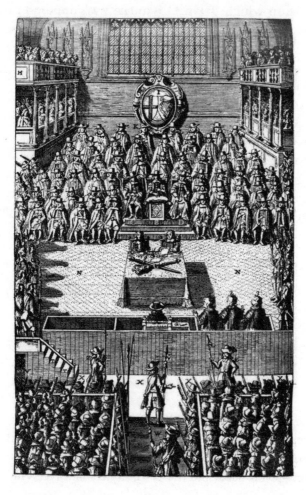

Trial of Charles I, 1688.

Quite apart from deprivation, he was subjected to cruel treatment as the following petition reveals:

1623: Brian O'Rourke addressed a Petition 'to the Lords and others of the Privy Council,

That being by their honours committed into the hands of Aquila Weekes, keeper of the Gatehouse, where he has remained the space of two years, having no means allowed him by the said keeper; so it was of late the said keeper gave command to his man to lay hands on the petitioner, and put him into a dungeon, where they manacled his hands to a post a whole night, and the morning following committed him close prisoner, not showing any warrant from them (the Lords) so that he still remained in daily fear of his life, being in the hands of such a cruel keeper. Prays therefore to be called before them to clear himself of those imputations which the said Weekes laid before them against him; and further that he might be removed to the Fleet, with an allowance for his maintenance, and that then the warden of the Fleet might report to them his carriage and behaviour.

Brian O'Rourke had apparently been transferred from the Fleet Prison to the Gatehouse Prison and petitioned to be returned to the former. By 1625, he had been moved permanently to the Tower of London.

The Plantation of Leitrim got underway from 1621 onwards. It involved investigation of title and measuring of land and incurred a great degree of dislocation in the division and apportioning of lands to undertakers, as well as the movement of settlers who would become tenants to the main beneficiaries, the undertakers. In the midst of all this upheaval the authorities were keeping a close eye on the O'Rourkes, in particular on Brian O'Rourke's younger brother Hugh. Lord Deputy Falkland saw him as a possible threat to a peaceable plantation. In 1625 he wrote to the Privy Council:

Some people have lately observed the conduct of Hugh O'Rourke, brother of him who is in the Tower, and the concourse of the people unto him where he resides, in or near the county of Leitrim. I wrote to him offering him money and letters of recommendation to the King and your Lordships, asking them to give him money for his maintenance in

England. But I prevailed not. He is a great figure, and if there are stirring times, the idlers of the Irish men of his country will be drawn to him. I desire to be to directed by your Lordships, and if you prepare a pension for him I will compel him to go over.

Apparently, there was some success in the matter of a pension, for a year later Lord Falkland wrote again:

I have sent over Con Mc Caffery O'Donnell and Hugh O'Rourke, younger brother to him that is in the Tower. His person speaks something for him. I have watched him and had him watched, and find his demeanour always fair, and though his religion is different, his conformity is not hopeless. He has no intention of flying to Spain.

A month later Lord Falkland thanks Lord Conway:

I am glad that you have provided well for Con O'Donnell and Hugh O'Rourke, as I requested. Their good position in England will have a good effect over here, as people thought they would be lost men, and imprisoned for life.

Knowing the fate of Brian O'Rourke, it is not surprising that rumours and fears for their safety would have been rife. A few days later in July 1626 the State Papers report:

Grant of a pension of £100 to Hugh O'Rourke, an Irish gentleman, for life, in the hope of his conformity and religion. He must first fully and clearly resign in the Court of Chancery all rights and title which he pretends to any lands in Ireland lately planted by British settlers.

Clearly none of this was acceptable to Hugh O'Rourke, either in regard to his religion, or in the surrender of his rights to lands. He was also possibly aware of the difficulties his brother had in receiving his pension. Like his brother and grandfather, he refused to bow to the inevitable. A few months later the King ordered his arrest but Hugh did what Lord Falkland had predicted he would not do: he flew to Spain.

In October 1626 Infanta Isabella wrote a letter to King Philip IV of Spain:

There is here a certain Hugo Ororque, an Irish gentleman, who says he is a grandson of the late Brian Ororque, Lord of Leitrim, and brother of the present Lord. He says his grandfather in 1588 sheltered 500 shipwrecked Spaniards, for which he was arrested and executed by Queen Elizabeth. In like manner one of Hugo's uncles, a son of the above Brian, co-operated with the League of Irish Catholics by supplying and maintaining 1,000 men until his death; and the actual Lord, his brother, is a prisoner in the Tower of London for the past seven years. Hugo's arrest has been ordered by the present King of England, but he managed to escape, and wishes to serve your Majesty in the War. Wants a grant corresponding to his birth, and Isabella recommends he should have same.

A few months later the Infanta received a letter from the Duke of San Lucar:

19 January 1627. Madrid.

It would be well that his Majesty should send the son of O'Rourke who lately fled from England and is a cousin of the Earl of Tirconnell, giving him some command, or some large grant; for he could immediately draw a whole countryside to the service of his Majesty.

Hugh O'Rourke had received a warm welcome at the Spanish Court and more than likely was given a command in the Spanish army. But at this point he vanishes from history. It is unlikely he ever returned to Ireland but lived his life as one of the many *émigrés* to the Continent. His disappearance to Spain did not augur well for his older brother Brian, who later that year made fresh appeals to the King, praying that 'all the evidence against him may be produced in a speedy trial, and that if acquitted he may have his liberty' It is ironic that at this same time, Brian's ex-guardian, the Earl of Clanricarde, was also petitioning the King, for non-payment of his £1,500, which had been promised in return for his relinquishment of Brian's wardship:

Petition of Richard, Earl of Clanricarde to the King, August 7 1626: He had given up the wardship of Brian O'Rourke in Leitrim, where King James I was going to make a plantation, and had received in return his promise of anything he liked in Ireland up to 1,500 pounds.

Despite further appeals, Clanricarde received no payment until almost twenty years after the promise was made. Both King James and Richard, Earl of Clanricarde were dead when in 1637, King Charles 1 wrote to Richard's son Ulick:

> 24 March 1637. Ordering that as his father gave up the wardship of Brian O'Rourke, the prime man of estate in Leitrim, in order to facilitate the Plantation of that country, and as he never got the 1500 pounds promised him in compensation, he shall now have that sum deducted from his composition for livery and fines of alienation made by his father, which is payable to the Court of Ward.

For a time, George Villiers basked in his good fortune and his future seemed secure. But during the 1620s, he became increasingly unpopular in England. While James I remained devoted to his favourite, the Privy Council were growing increasingly resentful of his power and privilege. They were acutely aware of the vast network of personal patronage and benefits he had amassed. Besides, he was notching up a series of blunders and military failures.

One of the more colourful of these was when he involved James's son Charles in a madcap adventure to Spain to try to secure the Infanta as a bride for Charles. They travelled incognito as Tom and Jack Smith, wearing false beards. The Spanish, more than likely highly amazed and sensing their upper hand in the situation, made extreme demands to safeguard her Catholic faith. Almost like prisoners in a foreign land, they were in the humiliating position of appearing to agree before they could return to England where they renounced the agreement. It was embarrassing but the besotted King called them 'my sweete boyes and deare ventrouse Knights worthy to be put in a new romanse'. Indeed James was prescient, for it inspired Alexander Dumas to model one of his *Three Musketeers* on George Villiers.

With distant memories of the Spanish Armada still persisting, England was highly relieved that the match had not succeeded. The country was more concerned with the cost of war, especially when failure was involved. In 1620 a crisis occurred, when Spanish Catholic forces invaded the Palatinate area of the Rhineland, ruled by the Protestant Elector Frederick, who was married to James's daughter Elizabeth. Though James was a pacifist and without funds for war, he had to present an image of champion to his daughter, and also as Protestant defender against Catholic incursion. Parliament voted to finance a land campaign into the Rhineland under Count Von Mansfield. The ships, carrying 12,000 reluctant conscripts from Dover, were struck with disaster in the form of a plague, which left only 3,000 weak and sickly survivors. The expedition had collapsed. It was the start of a pattern of failure that would dog future sea campaigns, and these would, crucially, be organised by George Villiers, Duke of Buckingham.

In 1625, the King, badly stricken with gout, died. He was entombed in Westminster beside the tomb of Queen Elizabeth, and that of his mother, Mary Queen of Scots. It was extraordinary that this event did not result in the eclipse of his favourite, George Villiers. When James's son Charles assumed the kingship as Charles I, he proved to be as loyal and supportive of the Duke of Buckingham as his father had been, very often to the detriment of his own standing at Court and in Parliament. They had shared that adventure to Spain and it is clear that Charles admired the dashing, virile Duke. Charles, in contrast, was diffident in manner and quiet of voice, and so small and slight in stature, that when Van Dyck painted him on horseback, he exaggerated his size in relation to the horse, in order to present him as a commanding figure. The Venetian Ambassador remarked in 1622 that he had found Charles 'caressing Buckingham like a brother and behaving as if the favourite were prince and himself less than a favourite.' He was of the opinion that it was to please the King, but clearly the two were firm friends, and when Charles became King, his loyalty to George Villiers annoyed and frustrated Parliament.

From 1625 onwards, however, the glittering career of Sir George Villiers, Duke of Buckingham was in trouble. He organised a sea expedition to Cadiz which ended in dismal failure, much to the fury of Parliament given the high cost of war. There was criticism of Buckingham's naval policy; the Spaniards had hurt English pride and revealed a loss of English maritime supremacy. There was also a sense of outrage over the excessive favouring of the Villiers family. The Parliament of 1626 made an attempt to impeach Buckingham. A declaration to the King stated, 'The principal cause of which evils and dangers we conceive to be the excessive power of the Duke of Buckingham and the abuse of that power.' The proceedings were not well handled and the impeachment failed due to a lack of evidence. It is interesting that it was at this time that he delayed the sealing of his Leitrim patent until December 1626, pending its ultimate transfer to his half-brother Sir William Villiers. His other half-brother Sir Edward, who had been involved in the Cadiz expedition, died in September of the dysentery that had swept through the troops of that ill-fated venture.

By the following year, the war offensive had spread to France, where some Protestant Huguenots had taken refuge. Parliament was not inclined to finance either English intervention in the Palatinate or sea operations against Spain or France. An extremely unpopular forced loan of over £200,000 was raised which enabled Buckingham to lead an expedition to France. In a badly planned attack he failed to take the French navy Atlantic fort, of Île de Rhé. This proved to be the last straw; he was pilloried by ballad-mongers and mocked in newsletters. Charles I, ever loyal, wrote to him anxious to take the blame for this disaster upon himself. Matters were reaching crisis point. Besides the hostility of Parliament and his countrywide unpopularity, there was a growing band of angry unpaid sailors who blamed him for their misfortunes.

In 1627, some of these dissatisfied sailors threw down the gateway of Buckingham's house. The King promised to give them their pay notwith-standing the reluctance of Parliament to grant money. They threatened to have the Duke's head on Tower Hill if this promise was not fulfilled. In April 1628 they crowded around the entrance of the House of Lords and Buckingham promised them fifteen months back-pay within a week. On 13 June, Buckingham's astrologer Dr Lambe was beaten to death by a mob. In August, he travelled to Portsmouth to assume command of the fleet in another expedition to relieve La Rochelle. On the morning of 23 August, John Felton, one of the angry seamen, bought a butcher's knife for ten pennies. In a quick stab to the heart he assassinated George Villiers, Duke of Buckingham. Charles, upon hearing the news, closed his eyes in pain, spoke no words but retired to his private chapel for hours. He was given a semi-royal burial in Westminster. Thus ended the life and career of George Villiers, Duke of Buckingham, at the early age of thirty-six.

In that same year, there was a petition from Brian O'Rourke to the Duke of Buckingham. He was fully aware that his estate had been acquired for plantation. There is a note of desperation in his plea:

Brian O'Rourke to the Duke of Buckingham: 1628
Protests his loyalty and objects that those who have got patents in the Plantation of his country have maligned him. His lands were granted to him by patents of 1604 in reward for blood lost in the Crown's cause. He

has been the King's ward, and daily begged to be allowed to sue out his livery, but this has not been permitted. He begs for liberty on any conditions, and offers to give security.

Now both James and the Duke of Buckingham were dead and Brian O'Rourke continued his life in prison. He was twenty-eight years old. He continued to make pleas for release but to no avail. Over the next ten years the lands of Breifne succumbed to the machinery of plantation with the arrival of settlers from England and Scotland. Twenty-one years after his incarceration he made his last plea. It was dated 8 January 1641, 'praying that he may be discharged and have the benefit of the law for the recovery of his estate'.

A few days later he was dead. The Burial Register of the Tower of London records his death, 'Brian O'Rorke, Irish prisoner, buried the 16th day of January, 1641.' He was forty-one years old and had been imprisoned from the age of twenty. The cause of death was not stated.

★ ★ ★ ★ ★

Less than a fortnight after the Duke's assassination, the estate of 6,500 acres of arable and pasture land and 5,114 of wood and bog in the barony of Dromahaire was transferred to George's half-brother William, by patent dated 5 September 1628. There were a number of stipulations. The lands were to be:

> ...held in capite by the service of one Knights fee and the rent of 83 pounds 6 *s* and 1*d* ... the premises being erected into the Manor of Dromahere with many large privileges, 2 weekly markets on Tuesday and Saturday and 2 fairs yearly on 10 July and 20 October at Dromahere, liberty to impark 1,000 acres with free warren, to export corn and other commodities growing upon the premises.

For this largesse, there was to be no obligation to reside on the property, for he was granted:

> ...[a] license of absence to him and his heirs ... discharging them of personal residence, on their keeping a sufficient agent upon the premises and to build within four years, a castle, 60 feet in length, 24 feet in breadth

and 32 feet in height with a bawn of 400 feet in circuit compassed with a stone wall 14 feet in height.

The building of Villiers Castle at Dromahaire commenced some time after 1628. It was of an unusual design – being based on a U-plan with stairs on the inside corners. Rolf Loeber offers the opinion that perhaps it was designed by John Johnson, who had been educated at Trinity and was both cleric and engineer. In 1622, he was appointed as minister and preacher for the vicarage of Dromahaire to take care of the religious needs of the new settlers. He resided in his parish of Killery, where he had a 'Tymber house' and other houses of office. Certainly in later years he was involved in architectural pursuits. Wentworth appointed him engineer over his palatial building at Jigginstown, Co. Kildare and he was also involved with the building of Carnew Castle in Co. Wicklow. By 1639 he had become vicar of Athenry.

Villiers Castle was built on the site of O'Rourke's sixteenth-century castle. It seems likely, as tradition has it, that the stones from this castle were used in the construction of Villiers Castle. The era of the Chieftain literally crumbled to build the new era of the Planter.

A few years after the assassination of George Villiers his widow Katherine, much to the dismay of King Charles, reverted to the Catholic faith and married Viscount Dunluce, the son of the Earl of Antrim. The King took charge of the Duke's children but eventually forgave her. Katherine's son George became the second Duke of Buckingham and proved to be as extravagant as his father George Villiers. He also inherited the good looks of his father; a songster of the times tells us:

No gallant peer by nature framed to warm
The lovely Fair could boast a nobler form

Like his father he also aroused feelings of animosity. Scandal was never far away; he was castigated in the House of Lords for his open liaison with the Countess of Shrewsbury, whose husband he had killed in a duel. He was attacked in the House of Commons for misusing public funds and conducting secret negotiations with France. He was gifted and clever; he produced a celebrated play, *The Rehearsal*, satirising the era's fad for heroic drama. This provoked the wrath of Dryden, who in turn satirised him as Zimri in the work *Absalom and Architophel*:

Was chemist, fiddler, statesman and buffoon.
Then all for women, painting, rhyming, drinking
Besides ten thousand freaks that died in thinking
In squandering wealth was his peculiar art
Nothing went unrewarded but desert.
Beggared by fools whom still he found too late
He had his jest and they had his estate.

He lost money defending himself against a trumped-up charge of sodomy. His accusers, one Philip Lamar and his mother, were found guilty of being suborned to swear the charge against the Duke. His reputation was ruined. When he died in 1687, his deathbed was described in Pope's *Moral Essays*:

In the worst Inn's worst room, with mat half hung
The floors of plaster, and the walls of dung
On once a flock bed but repaired with straw
With tape-tied curtains never meant to draw
The George and Garter dangling from that bed
Where tawdry yellow strove with duty red
Great Villiers lies

That account is disputed by another source which claims that he caught a chill after hunting and died at the house of one of his tenants at Kirkby Moorside in York, which 'neither is nor ever was an ale-house'. He was buried with due ceremony in Westminster Abbey. The lands of the O'Rourkes of Breifne would remain the property of the Dukes of Buckingham until the end of the eighteenth century, when they were sold to the Lane family of Lanesboro of Co. Roscommon. Villiers Castle in Dromahaire would end in ruins long before that time.

Plantation and the Rising of 1641

The Leitrim plantation got underway in the 1620s. Those who were granted lands were termed undertakers and their tenants were the settlers who moved in over the following years. Some of the major undertakers to receive land were Sir William Villiers at Dromahaire, Sir Frederick Hamilton at Manorhamilton, Henry Crofton at Mohill and Captain Robert Parke at Newtown (present-day Parke's Castle), all of whom built fortified residences. Of these, the larger-than-life Sir Frederick Hamilton would emerge as the most colourful and most detested character. Lord Deputy Wentworth described him as 'a gentleman of strange and extravagant humour'. At a later date, he managed to quarrel with many of his Protestant neighbours, including Sir William Cole of Enniskillen, Sir Robert Parke and Sir William Villiers.

Many of the undertakers already held property in Ireland. One such was George St John, nephew of Sir Oliver St John, the Lord Deputy (1616–1622). He had already been granted the castle of Carradrumruske (Carrick-on-Shannon) in 1619 together with twelve cartrons of land, now under the Leitrim plantation, he received an additional 400 acres. Sir Thomas Dutton who had previously received 1,000 acres in Longford now got a grant of 600 acres and Sir John King, who had obtained a lease on the Abbey of Boyle, received 800 acres in Leitrim – he later became an active land speculator. Captain Robert Parke was one of the

Parke's Castle. (*Photograph: Tommy Weir*)

military men who profited from their efforts when he received 1,000 acres of Con O'Rourke's land at Newtown. Another was Captain Henry Fortescue who was granted 1,500 acres and subsequently sold his land to Sir Frederick Hamilton. It appears that some of the smaller undertakers sold their land grant, possibly due to an inability, through lack of funds, to develop their estates. By 1641, the Villiers estate had increased in size to 8,000 acres and that of Sir Frederick Hamilton to 8,100 acres.

Protection of both undertaker and settler was an urgent priority in a country deemed a 'single and secure den of thieves'. The only border crossing of the Shannon with a fort was at Carrick Drumrusk (Carrick-on-Shannon) built in 1611. The task of building a fortified town to protect the area was contracted to Sir Charles Coote, Vice President of Connaught. Coote had already provided 'a fair large, wooden bridge leading over the Shannon'. Though he lived at Castle Coote in his estate in Co. Roscommon, he chose to site the town, which would be called Jamestown in honour of the King, in Co. Leitrim. He already had interests there, having set up the charcoal burning ironworks at Creevelea near Dromahaire at an earlier unknown date.

Jamestown Gate.

The only walled towns in Connaught at this time were Galway, Loughrea and Athenry. The specifications for the wall at Jamestown were very precise. It was to be:

> ...in compass upon the outside 160 perches, accounting 18 feet to the perch (equalling 960 yards, or an area of just over 11 acres); six feet and a half in breadth in the foundation, and fourteen feet high; to be six feet broad upon the top of the rampier, and thereon to be a parapet or battlement, six feet high and eighteen inches in thickness, the said wall and battlements to be made of good lime and stone.

Provision was also made for two gates and a water gate. Within the wall, the town was neatly planned with thirty-two plots for houses along two main streets which intersected. It was similar but much smaller than the other new towns such as Derry, Coleraine and Bandon. Its designer is unknown, but could possibly have been Nicholas Pinnar, the Surveyor General of forts, who had received lands in the Leitrim plantation.

This strong wall and fortification did not withstand the rebellion of 1641 and the town was taken by troops of the Confederate army in 1648. The walls remained until the mid-eighteenth century but by the nineteenth century only half of them were surviving. They gradually crumbled. A lorry crashed into the sole surviving gate in 1973, and the gate, despite public protest, was taken down.

To remedy the weaknesses of former plantations a number of conditions were drawn up in 1626. Some of them make interesting reading, 'Undertakers shall be compelled to reside on their estates in order to avoid the evils of absenteeism.' This stipulation was overlooked in the Villiers grant. Efforts to compel the natives to attend Protestant service must have been proving too difficult and unpopular, 'the clergy and officers of the Spiritual Courts shall not be allowed to molest the recusants or tax them heavily'. (There had been a fine of 12*d* for not attending Sunday Service.) Another stipulation throws light on existing farming methods, 'Instead of being fined for barbarously ploughing with horses tied by their tails to the plough, offenders shall be corporally punished.'

To further secure the safety of the settlers the King had written to the Lord Deputy in 1622, 'We have resolved to keep in Ireland a standing army of 5,000 foot and 500 horse ... the charge of which is to defrayed by the populace.' This was obviously much resented by the people for a direction was given, 'Soldiers shall not be allowed to march through the country alone or take money, but an officer shall go with them and take such food and drink as the populace can give and shall pay them with ready money or signed tickets.'

There is a record of a company of soldiers landing at Killybegs in 1626. They were under the command of Sir Charles Coote and were deployed to deal with rebels in Cavan, Longford and Leitrim. Unrest was bad in Leitrim where the process of plantation was widespread and thorough. In 1632 Lord Falkland wrote:

Humble remonstrances to be taken into consideration for the better securing of public peace in Ireland ... The chief of the O'Rourkes is now in the Tower, the best place for him. His brothers in Leitrim are angry that their lands have been planted. They should be looked to.

Even with Brian O'Rourke safely in the Towers and his brother Hugh in Spain the O'Rourkes were still a cause of concern to the authorities.

Manorhamilton Castle. (*Photograph: Tommy Weir*)

The most notorious Planter, Sir Frederick Hamilton, was the young-
est of seven sons of Lord Claud Hamilton, Dean of Dunbar, Lord of
Paisley Abbey in Scotland. His family was Catholic, related to the
Stuarts; his great-grandfather had been tutor to Mary Queen of Scots.
Frederick's brothers got lands in the Ulster Plantation in Tyrone and
Frederick was one of the first to receive lands in the Leitrim plantation.
In 1621 he acquired a grant of a quarter of land called Carrowross in
the Barony of Rosclogher, containing 788 acres of pasture and 2,612
acres of bog, and in the Barony of Dromahaire the quarter of land called
Knockevrohane containing 548 acres of pasture and 1,334 acres of bog
and wood – in all a total of 5,279 acres. In the Manor of Hamilton he
had the right to hold courts, to appoint judges and to hold a market on
Tuesdays and two fairs annually on 21 January and 22 September. He
undertook to build a castle with a bawn but there was a delay on this,
as Frederick spent some years abroad supporting the King of Sweden,
Gustaf Adolphus, in the Thirty Years' War. The castle was built in around
1634 of a granite-type stone and would prove to be one of the strongest
castles in Connaught. It was 105ft in length, 93ft in breadth, 40ft high

and surrounded by a bawn with flankers at four corners. It withstood attack in the rebellion of 1641.

Despite the size of his territory, Sir Frederick was keen to acquire more. A mere two years after his grant of 1621, he purchased an additional 3,310 acres from Captain Fortescue and was granted permission for a deerpark. Over the following years he increased his holding by a total of 6,307 acres of arable land and 10,050 of bog and wood. Some of the lands were in the Barony of Mohill. He inherited lands in Donegal, Derry and Tyrone, including the estate of his father-in-law, Sir John Vaughan. He also received Valentia Island in Kerry from Sir John Ans, a knight of James I.

In 1629, Sir Frederick cast his eye on some lands belonging to Sir William Villiers in Drumlease, Kiiannumery, Killargy and Clooclane. Apparently there was an agreement to purchase the lands for £4,000 but Villiers had second thoughts and offered Hamilton £100 to be released from the deal. Sir Frederick demanded £1,000 and for good measure brought a suit against Sir William Villiers. Proceedings were put on hold due to the illness of Sir William and his inability to travel to Ireland. He died in August 1629, just a year after the assassination of his brother George. Undaunted, Sir Frederick petitioned the King for the wardship of William's son George, so that when he would come of age he could fulfill his father's obligation. The King passed the case over to Sir Thomas Coventry, his Lord Keeper, possibly with a judicious word in his ear. Sir Thomas ruled against Hamilton and stated, 'as the case now stands it is impossible to dispose of the lands which the law has invested upon the heir within age and that therefore Sir Frederick must forego the hope of his bargain, although neither Sir William nor his lady is to blame for the matter'. He rather pointedly adds, that it is unfortunate for Sir Frederick that, 'he suffers for an act of God who took away Sir William's life'. A few months later in October, the King granted the wardship of George Villiers, 'son and heir to the late Sir William Viliers, to his mother Rebecca Villiers'. Coventry adds that, 'no enquiry shall be made into the performance or non performance of certain promises regarding building, etc. made when the Duke of Buckingham and Sir William Villiers got the lands now fallen to the latter's heir'. He further states that, 'no action shall be taken in consequence of the Duke having passed these lands to Sir William without licence of alienation'. The King's loyalty to his friend remained undiminished.

The settlers, who became tenants to the undertakers, were a mixture of newcomers who came directly from England and Scotland, and those who had come over in the course of earlier plantations. In Leitrim there was a steady drift of Scottish settlers from Ulster and Cavan – an extension of the Ulster Plantation. Some landlords provided houses on their estates for their settler tenants and some of the more substantial tenants built houses of their own with barns and outbuildings. There was a growth of plantation villages and towns such as Jamestown and Carrick-on-Shannon. There is a record of corn-mills and houses close to Manorhamilton and also of a Protestant minister James Stevenson in Leitrim who owned a house of his own and fourteen thatched houses. These were an improvement on the poorer native Irish dwellings described by Mc Lysaght:

> The cot was generally built on the side of a hill – usually raised three feet from the eaves to the ground on one side and the other side had a rock for a wall. The hearth is placed in the middle of the house and the fuel is made of earth and cow-dung dried in the sun. The smoke breaks through between rods and wattle.

These houses could be built in a day and had an earthen floor spread with rushes. At night the cow and hens were brought in for safety for fear of the fox and wolf.

The settlers introduced new farming techniques, such as the use of lime as fertiliser and English strains of cattle and sheep to improve the Irish stock which was considered to be very small in size. Some of the settlers were skilled tradesmen such as carpenters, tanners, masons, clothiers and smiths. In the area of Carrigallen and Ballinamore, Co. Leitrim, there is a record of one joiner, one tanner, one clay-potter, one felt-maker, one glover, one blacksmith. In Ballinamore, there were the brothers Thomas and Christopher Waller, who constructed a tuckmill, cultivated garden roots and supplied the full range of merchant wares described as 'wools, yarns, cloth, dying stuff and working tools'. At Sir Charles Coote's ironworks in Creevelea skilled immigrant workers were employed. A report by the Dutch *émigrés* Gerard and Arnold Boate state that Sir Charles Coote employed 2,500 workers at his smelting works in Cavan, Fermanagh and Leitrim. They add that of these workers some were English and the rest Dutch, 'because the

Irish having no skill in any of these things have never been employed — other than to dig it and do other labours'.

This Protestant entrepreneurship was in contrast to the position of the Catholic landowner, whose situation grew steadily more precarious through the 1630s. In Ulster, Longford and Leitrim, the lands of the Gaelic lords had been confiscated as part of the plantation. The native tenants had to move to higher, poorer lands while British tenants occupied the more fertile plains. Both the Catholic Lords and the native tenants watched their growing impoverishment with alarm. In the Dublin Parliament, the influence of the Catholic elite was reduced under the power of the new Lord Deputy Wentworth. They worried about their freedom to practise their Catholic religion and the plantation policies of Wentworth, who saw the extension of plantation as a means of securing loyalty. The question of tithes also caused a great deal of resentment. These payments of money to support the Protestant Church were compulsory for Catholics and Protestants alike. When the Dominicans and Franciscans reorganised in the 1630s, Catholics found themselves in the position of paying dues to both Catholic and Protestant Churches. This sense of grievance resulted in widespread support for the 1641 rebellion and in acts of violence meted out to Protestant clergymen.

It is a strange fact that the spark that set alight the 1641 rebellion came from Scotland. Trouble had erupted there four years previously over the matter of religion. The Scots felt that their Presbyterian religion was under threat by the religious policies of Charles I and Archbishop Laud. They had embarked on Church reforms, which the Scots, and indeed the Protestants in England, saw as favouring a return to Catholic practices. Soon Charles was involved in wars with the Scots and also in a mighty power struggle with the Parliament in England who did not share Charles's view of the divine right of kings. The situation became so bad that Wentworth prepared to utilise Irish Catholic troops to assist the King. This explains the thinking behind the Irish rebellion where the rebels claimed to act on behalf of the King.

The settler community was dumbfounded when suddenly, in October 1641, like the proverbial bolt from the blue, Sir Phelim O'Neill captured Charlemont, an important fort in Co. Armagh. It is a measure of their shock and dismay that Sir Toby Caulfield, commander of the fort, thought Sir Phelim was calling to have dinner. Sir Phelim was a Member of Parliament, as were some of the other leaders such as Philip O'Reilly in Cavan and Rory Maguire in Fermanagh. Sir Phelim claimed to have a commission from the King for his actions.

Though there was a military plan to capture Dublin Castle, the rebellion swiftly disintegrated into a popular revolt. Grievances and resentments burst forth in a number of terrible atrocities that panicked and terrified the Protestant community. Some examples make gruesome reading. At Portadown, a hundred Protestant settlers were herded onto a bridge, stripped and cast into the river Bann to drown. Those who attempted to escape were clubbed or shot. At Shewie, up to thirty settlers were locked into a house and burnt alive. The local leader here was a woman called Jane Hampson, described by a witness as 'formerly a Protestant but a mere Irish woman and lately turned to Masse'.

Atrocity.

There were numerous murders and killings throughout November and December of 1641. Reports and depictions of the atrocities appearing in London news-sheets caused outrage. Images of Protestants under attack entered the psyche of the Ulster Protestant community and contributed to the siege mentality that would persist for hundreds of years. Some tenants of Sir Phelim were attacked, including women and children. He was angry and told his followers, 'they have murdered my nurse and the child whom they knew my wife loved and respected and have brought out of England but I have beene revenged in them for I have hanged eight or nine of them for it'. This incident is indicative of the complex nature of the rebellion, as up until this time, there had been a good deal of interaction and co-operation between the native and settler community. The rebellion would soon spread through the country but it was Leitrim that first followed the lead given in Ulster.

The first salvo of the rebellion in Leitrim was fired when a group of insurgents, under the leadership of Colonel Owen O'Rourke and Con O'Rourke, attacked the ironworks of Sir Charles Coote at Creevelea, Co. Leitrim. Some eighty English were robbed before they fled for safety to the fort at Jamestown. The O'Rourkes, who had suffered so greatly in the recent plantation, were leading players in the revolt. They were joined by the McGowrans from Belturbet, Co. Cavan to form a force of about 200 men. They quickly took control of Leitrim except in the areas close to the forts of Jamestown, Manorhamilton, Newtown and Drumruske (Carrick-on-Shannon).

Kilmore House, home of the late Protestant Bishop of Elphin, was captured in a manner reminiscent of Sir Phelim O'Neill's taking of Charlemont. Rebel leader Laughlin Mc William O'Birne was admitted in a friendly manner by the bishop's widow, Mrs King. He promptly opened the gates and fired a shot to signal Con O'Rourke and Brian O'Birne who lay in ambush outside to enter. They took possession of the house and allowed the inhabitants to go to Jamestown. Some months later, in April 1642, troops from Jamestown failed in an attempt to recapture Kilmore House.

Such was the sense of grievance from the recent plantations and fear of the suppression of the Catholic religion that support for the action became widespread. It included the Catholic ruling elite (the clergy, priests and friars and even one Mc Sweeney, titular bishop of Kilmore) as well as the native population. Some soldiers who had been captains under the presidency of Connaught now joined forces with the leaders. As in Ulster, the rebels claimed to hold a commission from the King, 'to rob all the English but not the Scots or the Irish' on the grounds that 'they had rebelled in England and crowned a new King and intended taking the King prisoner'. Rumour and imagination led to Tirlah Mac Phelim O'Rourke reporting that, 'the King had given unto our O'Rourke, a prisoner beyond the seas, the whole county of Leitrim, and if they could not get the county they would try hard for the barony'. He was apparently unaware of the death of Brian O'Rourke in the Tower, almost a year earlier. Charles O'Rourke boasted that Dublin Castle had been taken and he claimed authority under the king's broad seal 'to take all the English men's goods and send them all away and that within eight days the said English were to depart for England or lose their lives'. Excitement and euphoria ran high in the early period of the insurrection and complete reversal of plantation policy appeared to be the goal. Property of the Planters was seized and destroyed and the rebels took to burning all things English – houses, farm buildings. Some rebels cast off their English-style clothing and donned Irish apparel.

The rebels regarded the Protestant settlers as heretics and certainly religion played a significant role in the rebellion in Leitrim. A later witness of the rebellion there would attest that attendance at Protestant service was 'a cause and matter sufficient for death'. He gave as an example the case of one Thomas McGranald who was hanged, 'notwithstanding he was of their own nation, but he went to Protestant church, and had lived amongst the English'. This was indicative of the bitter resentment of the Catholic community and their fear of the suppression of their religion.

Wild rumours said that under an Act of Parliament all Irish would be forced to go to Protestant service and that the English had plans to destroy all Irish Catholics. Settlers were cast off their lands but in some instances they were forced to choose between retaining their lands and going to Mass or losing their property. John Cooke of Mohill was offered his goods back if he would go to Mass and it was reported, 'to save his life is lately turned'. Another, Richard Ashe of the parish of Drumlaken, is 'gone from Protestant church to Mass'. Philip McMulmore O'Reilly who 'was very kind to the robbed and spoiled English' was derided as a 'Bodagh or Sasanogh' (Englishman).

Temple House, Sligo. (*Photograph: Annette Baesel*)

Settlers fled in fear to the safety of the forts of Jamestown and Drumruske. Other places of refuge included Castle Coote, home of Sir Charles Coote, Athlone Castle, and Templehouse – the castle of Sir William Crofton in Co. Sligo. Later, when Templehouse was besieged, William Oliphant, the vicar of Ballisodare and Enagh, was killed. His body was tied to a horse's tail, dragged through the district and buried in a ditch. He was praised by the settlers as a steadfast and loyal martyr, in contrast to Sir Henry Bingham, who was despised for attending Mass in Castlebar in the hope of retaining his property. The rebellion soon spread to Sligo and Mayo and quickly throughout other areas of Ireland. A feature of the rebellion was the number of 'loose and idle rogues' who took advantage of the breakdown in law and order to rob and plunder. Many of the settlers fleeing to Dublin were attacked and robbed. Ann Dudd of Ballinamore later gave evidence that her husband Richard Dudd was hanged by rebels near Dawlin's bridge in Co. Cavan, *en route* to Dublin. Elizabeth Vawse, widow of Robert Vawse, vicar of Carrigallen reports of others who, 'robbed of all they had, are now in Dublin in great want and misery'. The brothers, Thomas and Christopher Waller of Ballinamore were 'robbed of their goods'.

One refugee of interest was Julianna Johnson, wife of John Johnson, former vicar of Drumlease and reputed architect of Villiers Castle. In 1639 he was appointed vicar of Athenry, Co. Galway. Julianna gave evidence later that due to various robberies they lost goods to the value of £2,656, then at Christmas in 1641 her husband and son were killed in a skirmish at Inch, Co. Offaly. She fled with her nine small children and 'after much misery' reached Dublin.

Sligo was taken by a combination of Sligo and Leitrim rebels in December 1641. Amongst them were O'Connor Sligo and Brian McDonagh. Many of the Protestants were allowed safe passage to Boyle but there was a group of about forty who opted to stay. They were placed in Sligo Gaol for their own safety. On 13 January 1642, there was a drunken raid on the gaol by McDonagh and O'Hart accompanied by three or four butchers from the town armed with 'knives and skeans'. Almost all the inmates were killed. This massacre was to have serious consequences for the town of Sligo.

The stoutest resistance to the 1641 rebellion in Leitrim was mounted by Sir Frederick Hamilton. He was in Derry when news of the rebellion reached him. He set out immediately to return to his castle in Leitrim. One of his first acts was to erect a gallows outside his castle

Sligo Gaol. (*Photograph: Tommy Weir*)

walls. Soon he was hanging whatever rebels he could find thus earning himself the epithet 'Hanging Hamilton'. Apart from the advantage of his granite-walled castle he had an implacable determination to resist, and subsequently to command, fierce attacks of his own against the insurgents. As early as January 1642, he was holding Con O'Rourke and Connor Mc Laughlin prisoner in his castle. In an attempt to rescue them, the rebels offered an exchange of prisoners. Hamilton in reply, stated in a letter that he 'had rather they should die gloriously for the cause of Christ than I should so abase myself, as to deal with such traitors'. In an effort to take the castle, a rebel force under Col. Owen O'Rourke and Col. Con Mc Donnell O'Rourke aided by a force from Sligo under Brian McDonagh and the McGaurans of West Cavan, encamped at Lurganboy near Pound's Hill from where they had a view of Hamilton's Castle. The rebels seized Hamilton's cattle, burned his winter supplies of corn, and burned the town of Manorhamilton with its two corn-mills, forcing the inhabitants to flee within the castle walls. In reply, Hamilton had his prisoners Con O'Rourke, who was Col. Owen O'Rourke's brother, and Connor Mc Laughlin hanged outside the castle walls in view of the rebels. In reprisal, the O'Rourkes hanged a number of English prisoners, among them two Protestant ministers Wm Listen and Thomas Fullerton, who had been held at Dromahaire.

The rebels hoped to seize the castle on St Patrick's Day 1642, but first sent Hamilton a letter in an attempt to intimidate him into surrendering, warning that the castle was surrounded by 'great forces ... the strength of the county of Leytrim and from the Co. Mayo great supplies daily drawing towards so that you will find it impossible to resist'. In a robust refusal to do any such thing, Hamilton ends his letter with the words, 'I rest with contempt and scorn to all your base bragges, Your scourge if I can. F. H.' And so it was Sir Frederick Hamilton who marched out of the castle on St Patrick's Day and tried to provoke the rebels to attack by pretending to hang another prisoner, but it was nothing 'but an old sack of straw – long stockings being sown to it and thrown over the gallows'. The rebels remained in their camp, contenting themselves by seizing his plough-horses a few days later. Hamilton retaliated by stealing O'Rourke's cows and in the ensuing chase he succeeded in driving them from their camp.

Over the following months, Hamilton carried out a series of horrendous murdering raids. In April, in an attack on Dromahaire, he reportedly killed forty people, burned houses and took away over a hundred cows. A month later he was in Drumkeerin where he took the chief Mac a Nawe and his two daughters prisoner, burned houses and killed sixty people. One report, dated May 13 reads:

> This night we marched into the county of Fermanagh where we killed the wife of Donnogha Mac Flaherty Mac Guire, with about forty more whom we surprised in houses before day and brought with 9 score cows, above 200 sheep and goats and 47 horses and mares, 30 swine and five prisoners which we hanged.

The ferocity of his campaign appears to have kept the rebels quiet for the first half of 1642.

An interesting aspect of Hamilton's efforts against the rebels was the lack of support he received from his neighbours, Sir William Cole of Enniskillen and Sir Robert Parke of Newtown. Later Sir Frederick would lodge official complaints against Cole about his non co-operation during the rebellion, but in 1642 it was Sir Robert Parke who was the object of his ire. Parke, surprised and confused about the rebellion, like many of the undertakers, was determined to lie low within the castle walls and avoid confrontation with the rebels. When he inquired of the harper Dermot O'Ferry about the cause of the rebellion and was told they were acting in the name of the King he replied, 'we must all do as the King will have us do but until the truth of this appears, I will keep myself quiet'. He later added that he would defend himself 'till aid come without provoking or doing anything to draw the country upon myself'. In close proximity to the Leitrim and Sligo border, he nervously allowed the O'Rourke's cattle to graze next to his castle walls. When one of his soldiers attempted to steal some of them he was greatly alarmed and jumping from his bed exclaimed, 'now we are all undone' and ordered their immediate return.

It is easy to imagine Hamilton's attitude to this neutral position. When he decided on his major campaign – a direct attack on Sligo town – he was determined that Parke should help him. On 1 July 1642, he journeyed with his troops from Manorhamilton, stopped at Newtown and bullied Parke into joining him with twenty of his best soldiers. A short distance outside Sligo he halted and in an effort to rally his men, asked them if they had 'stomacks to attempt the burning of the town' and reminded them of the rebels there who had burned, attacked and sought their destruction. He ordered them to destroy all they could with fire and sword but not to loot. They advanced through the town, torching houses with their inhabitants; those who tried to escape were cut down with the sword. They attacked the Friary, destroying the church and their valuable chalices and 'all their superstitious trumperies belonging to the masse'. Many of the friars were killed; in all about 300 people of Sligo died. Hamilton only departed the blazing town on learning that Owen O'Rourke was advancing on Manorhamilton. The massacre of Sligo Gaol had been avenged.

Hamilton must have been displeased with Robert Parke's performance, or perhaps lack of it, for despite having been saved by Parke's men when he was unhorsed in an ambush on the journey home, he imprisoned Parke in Manorhamilton and disarmed his men. Astonishingly, this imprisonment lasted for a year and a half. Clearly Hamilton looked on Parke as a traitor and sympathetic to the rebels. Parke's father-in-law Mr Provie made representations to the Lord Justice who ordered his release. Hamilton at first ignored the order but was foiled by William Cole who arranged Parke's release while Hamilton was visiting Derry. Hamilton angrily accused Parke of openly consorting with the rebels. These accusations obviously carried no weight with the authorities, for Parke was restored to his castle and estates.

In fact, Sir Robert Parke was no different to many of the Protestant landowners who barricaded themselves in their castles and took no sides. In Castlebar, Sir Henry Bingham refused to protest for fear it would provoke an attack. Edward Crofton raised a troop of twenty horse and fifty foot for the 'better defence of his house and neighbouring garrisons'. William Crofton opened Templehouse near Ballymote to shelter refugees but mounted no attack on the rebels.

The antagonism between Sir Frederick Hamilton and William Cole came to a head in 1645 when Hamilton lodged official complaints against Cole. He accused Cole of repeatedly refusing to assist him during the rebellion; preferring to stay at home in Enniskillen, 'resting on a detestable neutrality, when great things could have been achieved for God and Parliament'. Cole stated that in July 1642 he had sent 400 men to aid Sir Frederick when the latter claimed he was surrounded and in grave danger. On arrival at Manorhamilton, it was clear there was no siege in progress and they were deployed to

Sir William Cole. (*Courtesy of the National Trust*)

mount an attack on Dromahaire. The following year, he himself had visited Manorhamilton with 500 men and, while attending the christening of Sir Frederick's son, had been subjected to many insults by Sir Frederick. Cole painted Hamilton as a cruel predator who antagonised his Protestant neighbours. His hounding of the gravely ill Sir William Villiers was still remembered and Cole accused him of coveting Sir Robert Parke's lands at Newtown. As an example of his cruelty to his fellow Protestants, Cole told how when Hamilton had burned Sligo, he had taken some Protestants into his protection. On discovering that two of them were John Wetterspin and his son James, who had earlier testified against Hamilton in a lawsuit, he promptly had John Wetterspin shot and had taken James to Manorhamilton where he was subjected to torture. Cole's sense of odium is conveyed in his comment that even the sight of 'his carriages made him extremely distasteful to men of all conditions that lived within twenty or thirty miles of him'. It recalls Wentworth's description of Sir Frederick as a 'gentleman of strange and extravagant humour' whose behaviour 'might pass in a Swedish army but in no civilized commonwealth'.

It was not until 1643, when Sir Charles Coote was commissioned to form a troop for Connaught that an official offensive was launched against the rebels. By that time, the English Parliament had taken over the control of Irish affairs by forcing the King to sign the Adventures Act, which, among other stipulations, prohibited the King from pardoning Irish rebels. It was an uneasy time for the Old Catholic English who had joined with the native Irish rebels in the Confederation of Kilkenny for the defence of Catholic rights. In 1642, the English Civil War broke out and the King was anxious to be at peace with the Confederation to help him against Scottish Presbyterianism. By 1645, Eoghan Ruadh O'Neill had returned from the Continent and with the Italian Archbishop Rinuccini, who arrived from Rome, they seized control of the Confederation. After an initial victory at the Battle of Benburb, again there was a failure to take Dublin.

Despite Frederick Hamilton's accusations of the lack of help it is clear that William Cole was active against the insurgents. In 1646 he requisitioned: £2000 for food; for 400 recruits clothed and armed; 400 swords; spades; 35 horses; 35 pairs of pistols, and ton of iron for mending the horseshoes and arms. He also sought £100 to repair bridges at Enniskillen and Ballyshannon. However, George Villiers remained absent. In August 1641, just before the outbreak of the rebellion, he wrote to the King begging 'to be excused for four years from the performance of the conditions specified in the Articles of plantation and that he need not reside on his estates provided he always keep an efficient agent there'. When Sir Charles Coote was co-ordinating the offensive against the rebels he used Villiers Castle to quarter some of his troops. In April 1646, a clearly worried George Villiers sent a petition to the king:

Sir George Villiers has a valuable and strong house in Leitrim at Dromahaire on the borders of Co. Sligo. He fears that the rebels may occupy it as Sir Charles Coote has had to withdraw the garrison from it to keep the field. He prays that Philip Taylor may be commissioned to raise a company of dragoons or firelocks and that half of them may be ordered to remain at Dromahaire where he will provide for them. The Lord Lieutenant to be told of this.

Sir Charles Coote possibly had diverted his troops elsewhere to tackle the new dynamic of O'Neill and Rinuccini in control of the Confederates. It seems likely that at some date between the writing of this letter and the arrival of Cromwell in 1649 that Villiers Castle was indeed destroyed. The 'strong house' had lasted less than twenty years. Today it remains an impressive ruin.

There is also confusion over the exact date of the destruction of the castle at Manorhamilton. One account published in 1662 states that it took place in 1641 when Sir Frederick, intent on revenging the death of his son while on a foraging raid in Roscommon, tricked some Irish chieftains to dine with him in the castle. The account goes on that he 'hanged them after dinner and caused their thighs to be broken before execution'. In retaliation, the neighbouring Chiefs attacked and burned the castle. The dinner murders are mentioned in other accounts and in local oral tradition but his son's death took place in 1647 and Sir Frederick was at large himself during the 1640s. Patrick G. Smith in his book *Wild Rose of Lough Gill* dates it to 1643 when Owen Roe O'Neill, helped by the Irish of Sligo and Breifne, gained admission to the castle with the aid of a simpleton, Murty McSharry, who led them through an unguarded entrance. They sacked and burned the castle leaving Sir Frederick watching the blaze from Saddle Hill, four miles north of Manorhamilton. In another version, Gilbert's *Contemporary History of Affairs in Ireland* places the date as 1652 quoting from a seventeenth-century account:

> ...some Connaughtmen that would not adhere unto Clanrickard other than under the shelter of the Connaught forces, did join with Ulster now together commanded a partie to Hametowne, a strong and commodious place in the Barony of Rosclogher in Dartrienaglanties which was surprised. The garrison happninge to be all abroade, the partie cominge

between them and home, killed them, intred the same, rich and plentifull of both provision and ammunition, covered with leade a most necessarie ware for that armie, made havocke of all, rifled the house and demolished two or three garrisons...

Finally, O'Donovan in his Ordnance Survey Letters for Co. Leitrim (1834) says, 'His castle is said to have been set on fire by a family of McLoughlin, who detested his name and his power. After the burning of his castle he passed over to Scotland where he shortly died of a lousy disease.' Sir Frederick did indeed die in Scotland in 1647. Hamilton had made so many enemies that it is entirely apt that the list of suspects for the destruction of his castle would be numerous.

It would appear that the period from the mid-1640s to the mid-1650s saw the destruction of Villiers Castle, Manorhamilton Castle and Parke's Castle. The walls of Jamestown were breached by the Confederates in 1648 and the town taken. By 1649 however, the Confederacy had weakened with dissension between Rinuccini and the Old English Catholics.

Rathcline Castle. (*Courtesy of Lord Rossmore and the Irish Architectural Archive*)

Rinuccini departed for Rome in 1649 and Owen Roe O'Neill seemed unable to make further headway.

In England, a very bloody civil war had ended with the execution of Charles I in January 1649. Charles wore a second shirt to the scaffold, to prevent any shivering in the January air to be mistaken for fear. The forces of Parliament had triumphed. It was imperative that Ireland must be subdued. Oliver Cromwell, who had emerged as the toughest military leader of the Parliamentary troops during the civil war, accepted command of the expedition to crush the Irish revolt. England was concerned not so much with Confederates, as with the Royalist, largely Protestant army, that had come to the fore led by the Duke of Ormonde. Cromwell arrived with thirty-five ships carrying 12,000 troops. He stated:

> We come to break the power of lawless rebels who having cast off the authority of England live as enemies to humane society ... we come (by the assistance of God) to hold forth and maintain the lustre and glory of English liberty in a nation where we have an undoubted right to do it.

He carried out his plan with missionary zeal with the slaughter of thousands of rebels and civilians in Drogheda and Wexford. In a ferocious and bloody campaign, Cromwell succeeded in subduing Ireland and revenging the revolts of 1641.

The Age of the Landlord:
1800–1906

George Villiers, Duke of Buckingham, sold his Irish estates in 1710 to the Lane family of Rathcline Castle, Tulsk, Co. Roscommon. Captain George Lane had been granted the lands in Roscommon for his military services by a grateful Queen Elizabeth. He had fought in the Battle of the Curlews when Sir Conyers Clifford was slain by Brian Oge O'Rourke. He had also taken part in the Battle of Kinsale. The Lane Family remained Royalist supporters but managed to retain their estates during the Cromwellian plantation. When Charles II was restored to the throne, George Lane's grandson also called George became 1st Viscount Lanesborough. The addition of the lands of the Villiers estates increased their properties considerably. On his death, the estates passed to his son James, 2nd Viscount Lanesborough, who became an absentee landlord when he moved to London with his wife Mary. They built two houses, one in Golden Square Westminster and the other at Hyde Park, now known as the Lanesborough Hotel. They had no children and when James died, all his properties were inherited by his half-sister Frances. Frances was the widow of Viscount Galway who was killed at the battle of Aughrim supporting King James. When Frances Lane married Mr Henry Fox of Yorkshire it was the start of the long stewardship of estates in Ireland by the Lane-Fox family of Bramham Park, Yorkshire. Her brother James Lane, 2nd Viscount Lanesborough, had stipulated in

Bramham Park. (*Courtesy of Nicholas Lane-Fox*)

his will that the Lane name and family crest should be retained and initially the surname was Fox Lane rather than Lane-Fox.

In 1710, the year the Lane family acquired the Villiers estate, Robert Benson, 1st Lord Bingley began the construction of Bramham Park over in Yorkshire. It was built in the style of a Florentine villa of the sixteenth century, inspired by his travels in Italy during his Grand Tour of Europe. French-style gardens after Le Notre surround the house with parkland, ponds and woods. His daughter Harriet, married to George Fox Lane, added ornate temples. When she died without heir, the house was occupied by her half-sister Mary Goodricke for a period of twenty years. This tenure caused a decline in the fortunes of Bramham Park and it was despoiled of household silver, stone garden ornaments and a 'fine oak wood'. On her death in 1792, the estate passed to James Fox, nephew to Harriet and George Fox Lane. It was James who was responsible for changing the surname from Fox Lane to Lane-Fox. There is a family joke that as a keen hunting man he preferred the idea of a Lane chasing a Fox! It is likely that he felt the emphasis should be on his own surname and indeed in most of the correspondence with his Irish stewards, he is referred to simply, as Mr Fox. He was MP for Horsham, Sussex and married Marcia Lucy, daughter of George Pitt, 1st Lord Rivers. No doubt while James was preoccupied with restoring Bramham to its former glory, he was also worried about his estates in Ireland.

The 1790s was a period of turmoil in Ireland. In Ulster there had been violent clashes between the Protestant secret society, the Peep O' Day Boys and their Catholic counterparts, the Defenders. Soon groups of Defenders were forming in North Connaught. In Leitrim many of the poorer sections of society joined them. It was a secret oath-bound society, which at first had no political agenda. They dealt mainly with local grievances regarding land and the payment of tithes, which Catholics had to pay to the Established Protestant Church. Their activities included attacking and burning houses and barns, destroying crops and maiming cattle. In 1793 England was at war with France and the Government proposed to set up a militia in each county – Leitrim was to supply some 300 men. Local Defender groups in Leitrim were outraged and there were some fierce clashes between them and the militia at Carrick-on-Shannon and Drumkeerin. In 1795, there was a very decisive victory for the Government forces at Drumcollop. Despite large numbers, the Defenders were poorly armed and lacked military skills. Troops were drafted into Leitrim and the society was put down in a fierce onslaught with wholesale arrests, torture and hangings. Large numbers were sent to sea to join in the war with France. The countryside was quiet. Small wonder then, that when the 1798 Rebellion of the United Irishmen sparked off rebellions in Dublin, Kildare, Meath, Wicklow and most notably in Wexford, there was no uprising in Leitrim.

The 1798 Rebellion, fired by the ideas of the French revolutionary ideals of republicanism, liberty and equality, was doomed from the start through the arrests of the leaders and lack of co-ordination. The French had promised help to the rebellion in Ireland and in August 1798 General Humbert arrived from France with three ships at Killala, Co. Mayo. Humbert famously succeeded in routing the Government's army under General Lake at Castlebar. Following this victory, Humbert hoped to meet up with the rebels in the midlands. Having been told that the country around Lough Allen and Carrick-on-Shannon was 'very well disposed' he decided to take a route through Leitrim. At Colooney they were attacked by militia from Sligo under Col. Charles Vereker.

Teeling Monument,
Collooney.
(*Photograph:Tommy
Weir*)

Largely due to the actions of his aide-de-camp, Bartholomew Teeling,
Humbert again won the day though many of his soldiers had been
wounded. He set off for Ballintogher and from there to Dromahaire.
They had few horses and were heavily laden with cannon and guns
and forced to haul the ammunition wagons manually. The journey
from Ballintogher to Dromahaire, a distance of nine miles, took eleven
hours. Dispirited and exhausted they rested at Dromahaire where they
received support and sustenance. Humbert dumped some cannon and
tumbrils into the River Bonet close to Dromahaire. They headed for
Drumkeerin where they were treated to their first cooked meal in
many days. One of the French later paid tribute to the friendly people
of Leitrim. Significantly, only about 500 Leitrim men joined to assist the
soldiers led by Humbert. This was in contrast to the thousands involved
in the clashes just three years previously at Drumcollop. Humbert and
his army, when faced with the combined armies of General Lake and

Cornwallis, were forced to surrender at Ballinamuck, Co. Longford on 8 September 1798.

One important result of the 1798 Rising was the realisation by the Irish Parliament of the Protestant Ascendancy that their best hope for survival lay in a union with Great Britain – something long advocated by William Pitt. On 1 August 1800 the royal assent was given to an Act of Union which came into being on 1 January 1801. Ireland would now be governed from Westminster with Irish MPs travelling to London to represent Ireland. The old Parliament House at College Green, Dublin would cease to function.

A few years before the Rebellion, a French traveller through Connaught was shocked by the apparent poverty of the people. Their huts seemed not fit for habitation and their nakedness was 'most unpleasant'. However, he was surprised at their healthy appearance which was due to their diet of potato and for which he stated they had a 'singular respect'. In 1802 a Statistical Survey by M'Parlan commented on the poor soil and drainage of much of the land of Leitrim and went on to state that the 'coldness, the clamminess and wet of the soil require the vegetative inspiration of heat to be productive'. Indeed so stiff and unyielding was some of the soil in Leitrim, that a special implement was made to enable the planting of the essential potato. It was called a steeven and was described as follows:

It is made of a pole about four feet long, and three inches in diameter, within about nine inches of the lower extremity, which tapers to a point; a resting and working place is fixed for the foot, to press the steeven into the potato ridge. Into a hole thus made, the potato-cut is let fall, then the mould, and so work away.

M'Parlan reports on the limited amounts of grain grown in Leitrim.

The only variety of grain, except oats, for which there is general abundance for home consumption extends to a little barley, less rye, and still a lesser quantity of wheat, and those only in a few demesnes of a few residing gentlemen, or a few pet fields of very few farmers.

In 1831, Robert Stewart, agent of the Lane-Fox family, reported on the use of the spade and especially the implement called the loy:

...it is hardly credible to any person who has not been an eye witness of it, the quantity of land that is turned up by that tool – much has been said and written in England about spade husbandry, but those who are advocates of that plan have only to spend the months of April and May in Ireland where they will see that system with its miserable results in full operation.

In the early nineteenth century there was a dramatic increase in the population of Leitrim. In 1821 the census shows a figure of 124,785. This figure rose to 141,303 in 1831 and by 1846 had risen again to 155,297. Today the population of Leitrim is approximately 28,000, so the numbers of the pre-famine years are difficult to grasp or visualise. Providing adequate housing for this rapidly expanding population was difficult if not downright impossible. In the same report of 1831, Robert Stewart described the people's solution to the problem:

In the pretence of building a new cattle house or barn they put up a mud hovel, and no sooner is it up, than either the new or the old is occupied by a married son or a married daughter or some other undertenant who gets a portion of the land and who cannot again be displaced without the greatest difficulty.

Leitrim had a vast rural community, as the few towns such as Carrick-on-Shannon, Carrigallen, Mohill, Ballinamore and Manorhamilton, according to M'Parlan, contained about eighty houses most of them very small. He mentioned that the number of smaller villages such as Drumshanbo, Drumkeerin and Dromahaire numbered about thirty to forty houses.

A good picture of this rural community is described in a report sent to James Lane-Fox in 1818. Earlier that year he had confessed to his agent James Shanley, 'I do not think that I have ever felt at ease concerning my Irish properties.' He decided to commission an independent inquiry about his estates in Ireland. The estate in Leitrim was the largest holding of the Lane-Fox family, who also held land in Waterford, Longford, Roscommon and Dublin. By this time it comprised some 17,296 acres, described as of 'various kinds of soil, some stony parts and others deep rich land with part bog and mountain'. It was let to about twenty-five tenants and the rents amounted annually to £4,928 8s 1d. Many of these tenants, who subdivided the land and rented to a great number of undertenants, became known as 'middle-men'. These middle-men were inclined to charge higher rents than the landlord and to treat the subtenants harshly. In effect the landlords were deprived of revenue from their own estates. The estate was managed by an agent, at this time James Shanley, who collected the rents and forwarded them to England.

The report made grim reading. It describes in vivid detail the abject poverty of the people, their exploitation by the middle-men, the poor farming practices and the desolate aspect of the countryside. Some extracts paint the picture:

> Potatoes is the only food they eat along with butter-milk and a few eggs. The farmers are in general clothed in rags without shoes and stockings (but) are seemingly a stout hardy set of people ... The under-tenants live in wretched houses built of mud and sod walls and covered with thatch and in general without chimneys and with the exception of three or four houses not a range or grate on the estate. The chief crop is potatoes planted 2 years and after them 3 crops of oats and the land at that time comes filled with various weeds that no more corn crops can be procured from it and they then let it out to grazing. They leave it to grow weeds for several years until the slow movement of time return it to crops which is generally upward of twenty years and it is at that time ready for the same plan to be pursued on it again ... The only implements they use are the spade, shovel and rake as the plough is unknown amongst them. The fences are sod walls and great ditches without a tree in any fence and the only wood on the estate are a few trees planted around some of the houses by the tenants. The late bad times along with the high rents the middle-men have extracted from them have nearly reduced both the occupiers and the middle-men to a state of beggary.
>
> Mr Shanley has had great difficulties ... not having the aid of a plan or book of the estates and unless a new arrangement is made the estate in a short time will be left with nothing but a population of paupers on it – the tenants. I have no doubt if they had their farms set out and each man had his part to himself that a few years would restore that confidence which ought to exist betwixt landlord and tenant and without which no estate can prosper or be improved.

It is obvious that the improved husbandry at work in England and in some parts of Ireland, following the Agricultural Revolution, had not reached this part of Leitrim. Nor had the countryside recovered from the felling of the woods in the previous centuries. The undertenants had been reduced to a state of inertia as any attempt at improving their holdings invariably led to an increase of their rents by the middle-men.

Though the Lane-Fox family were absentee landlords, a term that later became synonymous with neglect and exploitation, they took a keen interest in their estates and kept in close touch with their agents who supplied frequent reports. There is evidence of a strong sense of duty and a great deal of goodwill. The independent study of his estates was a cause of anguish to the landlord James Fox. He penned an impassioned letter in response to the report, venting his fury at the middle-men. He was vehemently opposed to the practice of subdivision, where holdings were divided into increasingly smaller parcels of land. He felt sacrifices would be required and said:

> I owe them to my family and successors, to the welfare of my country and the cause of humanity. It is my decided opinion and resolution to grant no leave of a single acre except to the real occupier and if any getting a leave from me should re-let any part to another I will a clause expressly affirming that his leave shall be void, by which means I hope to get rid of that real scourge of the Irish and their country and procure myself the blessings of many thousands. Those estates already out of leave, I am sure from what I have heard of your sentiments, I need not recommend to you not to lose an hour in taking the safest and most effectual measures to redeem from the tyranny and ruinous system of the middle-men.

He saw 'the rooting out of the middle-men as the only means to gain the heart of the people and to keep them in attachments to this country'.

Evidently, James Shanley was somewhat overwhelmed by the difficulties involved and had not replied, for two months later James Fox received a letter from his solicitors at Lincoln Inn Fields expressing surprise that Mr Shanley had not acknowledged the letter but pointing out that:

> ...the getting rid of the middle-men cannot be quite so expeditionary attained as you may perhaps imagine, for they must all have regular notices to quit their holdings before any new regulations or change

of system can be adopted. We always considered those middle-men as oppressive and ruinous and the only reason for continuing them was that by so doing the people were well secured but it now appears from experiences that that reason has entirely failed and therefore it seems high time to put an end to the system altogether as well for the interests of the landlords and the improvements of their estates as for the good of the country.

In 1819, a year after receiving the dismal report, James Fox sold the lands in Longford and Roscommon to Mr Luke White for £74,000 and retained the estates in Waterford and Dromahaire. From then on he became one of those improving landlords who administered their estates through an agent or steward. Throughout the 1700s, at the peak of the Protestant Ascendancy, landlords sought to model their estates in the English fashion, planting trees, building roads and creating villages. They also tried to improve farming practices. It was out of such ideas that the village of Dromahaire grew. James Fox and his son George Lane-Fox, who succeeded when he died in 1821, were very personally involved in the development of their estates. While unable to effect a miracle in the pattern of landholding, they embarked on a series of improvements, which over the years gradually changed the appearance of the countryside.

The question of roads was an urgent priority for it was noted in a report on the estate that there was 'a want of roads which made a lot of it inaccessible to any wheeled carriages and in many places even to horses'. David Stewart succeeded James Shanley as agent. He was certainly a most capable man. In 1831, a house called the Lodge was put at the disposal of the agents. Initially it was a long, low, thatched building close to the ruins of Villiers Castle. It was there that the Lane-Fox family stayed on their trips over to Ireland. Both agents worked hard to develop the estate. David Stewart did not have a very good view of the local tenantry when he wrote in 1832, 'the habits and temper of the people are certainly a serious drawback, yet I cannot help thinking that much may be done with them, wild as they are, by treating them with firmness, justice and conciliation'. A major road-building and tree-planting campaign was set in motion. The brothers Thomas and Joshua Kells who worked for George Lane-Fox at Bramham Park were frequently sent over to inspect progress. In 1831, Joshua, who would later succeed as agent at Dromahaire, wrote to George Lane-Fox saying, 'I am very agreeably surprised with Dromahaire … it is certainly very beautiful and only wants a little planting in different directions to make it complete.' His brother Thomas reported some time later:

> You would be very pleased to see the improvements about the village. Altogether the people look much more comfortable and keep their places cleaner. Most of them have flower gardens before their windows – some have a show of dahlias. It is quite delightful to see it. Mr Shanley says they are much fonder of attending to their gardens of flowers than to paying their rents. I am happy to say they all seem very well disposed – a very fine estate … There were no fewer than fifty persons attending your Dispensary yesterday for medical advice. I am sorry to say the weather is very wet and the corn is rotting in the ground.

The dispensary had been set up and continued to be subsidised by the Lane-Fox family. It was a great boon for Dromahaire and outlying areas, as a report in 1841 of the Poor Law Commissioners stated, that there

The old dispensary, Dromahaire. (*Photograph: Tommy Weir*)

were just seven dispensaries in the county, each with an area of at least 20,218 inhabitants to cater for and complained of the long distances people had to travel for medical help. Again one is struck by the vast numbers of the population. Only a small proportion of them could be catered for in the dispensaries, and the report said as much, 'the district of each is too large and too populous'. The report adds that while Leitrim had a population of 155,297 inhabitants, the county infirmary had accommodation for only thirty-one males and fourteen females. James, and later his son George, endowed the Church of Ireland churches in Dromahaire and Killenummery and several schools.

A census taken on 14 April 1831 shows a population of 420 in Dromahaire. Some of the names include Hugh Gillmor, William Robinson, Edward Hozey. The Gillmor family began trading in Dromahaire in 1820 and still continues to trade there almost 200 years later. The Hozey family set up the mill in Dromahaire and the Robinson family were also business people. Other names listed were William Martyn, Bart Somers and Arthur Kilmartin.

Two years later, in September 1833, Joshua Kells reported that he had a very pleasant journey across to Waterford and then to Dromahaire by the *Sligo Mail* and:

> ...reached this place on Thursday. I have made a beginning to collect the rent and so far I am happy to say they have paid very well. I have seen Mr. Stewart's new line of roads which are very beautiful and when finished will make a great improvement to the estate. A great deal has been done on roads.

But matters were not quite as tranquil as described. Two months later, he would write of a disturbing event at the Lodge. There was a political background to the incident.

Following the failure of the 1798 Rebellion and the subsequent Act of Union binding England and Ireland, there was an uneasy peace in Ireland during the early 1800s. It was the era of Protestant Supremacy and Catholics were excluded from Government. The rising middle class of Catholic merchants and lawyers grew increasingly resentful. Daniel O'Connell, a Catholic and a brilliant lawyer, emerged as the leader of a mass movement dedicated to the cause of Catholic Emancipation. He was entirely opposed to the use of violence which

George Lane-Fox (The Gambler). (*Courtesy of Nicholas Lane-Fox*)

he found abhorrent. Instead his followers were encouraged to march like soldiers, four abreast in long orderly lines to the polling booths and vote for the candidate who favoured Catholic Emancipation. This was in defiance of the traditional practice of voting as dictated by their landlord. Encouraged by the Catholic clergy and fired by O'Connell, the campaign was very successful and won its first major victory in Waterford.

The Waterford Election of 1826 caused a great deal of consternation to George Lane-Fox, who held an estate in Waterford, as indeed it did to the landlord class throughout Ireland. The forty-shilling freeholders had always voted according to the instruction of their landlords. Voting was public and to do otherwise was to risk eviction or some form of penalty. Lord George Beresford, son of the Marquis of Waterford and brother of the Church of Ireland Archbishop of Armagh was one of the most powerful proprietors in Ireland. He was the expected winner of the election. O'Connell urged instead a vote for Villiers Stuart a twenty-three-year-old Protestant who favoured Catholic Emancipation. Organised into marching groups wearing green ribbons and cockades and accompanied by priests and bands, the forty-shilling freeholders defied their landlords and Villiers Stuart carried the day. It was a major blow to the Protestant Ascendancy. David Stewart wrote a letter to George Lane-Fox giving his views on the affair:

> I communicated your views to your tenants at Dromahaire and stated to them the absolute necessity of their adhering to the interests of so kind and excellent a landlord. I at the same time stated that the Waterford tenants had been treated by you with the utmost kindness and generosity, that they had promised and expressed the strongest desire to attend to their landlord's wishes in the ensuing election at Waterford. I also stated that I knew that the priests were opposed to Mr Fox's views and that in the event of the Waterford tenants acting in the way they proposed and promised you would feel disposed to grant them leases on fair terms and that in each case you would also feel disposed to trust the Dromahaire tenants – one and all declaring that you could depend on them to a man. The Waterford tenants had declared the very same and made the strongest protestation that you might depend on them to support your friend. The Election however came and you now know the result. I must however state that I do not think the tenants were altogether to blame as I thought at the time that had you or even myself been at Waterford the tenants would in my opinion have voted for your friend in defiance of the priests. I have good grounds for this opinion ...
> In the event of another election your tenants will vote as you wish them provided either you, Mr Kells or Mr Shanley or myself be there to guide them not withstanding the monstrous influence of the priests.

This was wishful thinking on the part of David Stewart. Two years later Daniel O'Connell, though a Catholic, went forward himself and won a resounding victory in the Clare Election of 1828. It resulted in the passing of the Catholic Emancipation Act of 1829 which admitted Catholics to Parliament.

George Lane-Fox was possibly none too pleased but was at this time preoccupied with a disaster at Bramham Park. In July 1828, while the family was away at a funeral, the house caught fire. A man galloped to Leeds to summon the fire brigade while the estate workers fought the blaze. Unfortunately the house was gutted and many treasures of Lord Benson were lost. George Lane-Fox was nicknamed 'The Gambler'. He was a colourful character and larger than life in many ways; he was 6ft 5ins tall and in later life weighed as much as nineteen stone. He social-

Georgina Lane-Fox. (*Courtesy of Nicholas Lane-Fox*)

ised with the drinking and gambling circle of the Prince Regent. There is irony in the fact that the efforts of the firefighters were hampered when a new billiard table jammed the doorway. His wife Georgina, described as witty and pretty, was very extravagant and kept a salon in London. Like today, she did not escape the notice of the gossip column-ists and was referred to by the contemporary diarist Thomas Creevey as the 'notorious Mrs Lane-Fox'. She was eventually paid off with a hefty settlement. George's father James had bailed him out several times. After the fire the family, unable to rebuild due to the crippling gambling debts, moved into houses on the estate. Bramham remained a ruin for the next eighty years.

Reverberations from the fight for Emancipation were echoed in a disturbing incident at the Lodge in 1833. David Stewart had called a meeting of the larger tenants of the estate, the local magistrate, and both Catholic and Protestant clergymen to outline changes in the terms of landholding on the estate. In a manner reminiscent of O'Connell's organised marches, a group of between 300 and 500 men in regular order, four abreast arrived at the Lodge, but unlike O'Connell's marchers, they were armed 'with guns and pistols, pitchforks and sticks'.

Joshua Kells wrote a letter to his brother at Bramham:

> ...you may easily imagine our surprise and alarm at this most extraordi-
> nary attack ... [they] caught hold of his collar [Mr Stewart's] evidently
> with a view to drag him to the crowd and I have no doubt the conse-
> quences would have been serious ... not until they began to expect a party
> of police did they begin to disperse ... we have since been guarded by a
> party of police and the yeomanry, who are principally Mr Fox's Protestant
> tenants and acted in the best possible manner ... I must observe to you
> that most of the ruffians were strangers but there is no question they were
> brought there by some of the tenantry several of whom I believe were in
> the crowd ... now I hope they have seen the error of their ways ... I hope
> Jane will not hear of this although it will no doubt soon be in the newspa-
> pers ... it will make her very uneasy.

It is unclear what precipitated the demonstration but the tenants obviously were objecting to some changes in the terms of their landholding.
All accounts concentrate on the details of the 'outrage'. David Stewart
wrote his own account at the Lodge in Dromahaire and sent it to the
Government:

> On Thursday 31st October 1833 I had occasion to call together the ten-

The Lodge.
(*Photograph:
Tommy Weir*)

ants of George Lane-Fox Esq. in order to explain to them the various regulations proposed by Mr Fox for their benefit and introduced into effect under my direction.

The tenants were requested to meet about 11 o'clock and about that hour many of them assembled but many were still absent and the business of the meeting was postponed in order to give those absent time to arrive at the Lodge and whilst we were in this state about 1 o'clock or between 12 and 1 o'clock a large body of men 300 or so, many of them armed marched over the Bonet by the bridge of Dromahaire, passed in at the iron gates belonging to the Lodge and gave several loud cheers and horrible yells. After which they instantly surrounded the Lodge, took possession of all the gates and placed sentinels with muskets and other arms at each gate and refused admittance to all persons whom they considered an impediment to their proceedings and prevented any person passing out.

After this they demanded admittance into the Lodge and repeatedly knocked at the doors both at the back and front of the Lodge and tried by every means in their power to force them open, demanding that I should go out to meet them and expressing their determination to drag me out by force if I would not comply with their demands. At this time there were upwards of forty persons in the Lodge many of them amongst the most respectable of Mr Fox's tenants and some neighbouring gentlemen. There were also Roman Catholic clergymen and two of the Protestant clergymen in the Lodge, one of them is a magistrate. The clergymen of both persuasions and also the gentlemen exerted their utmost influence to moderate the fury of the mob by reasoning with them and pointing out the consequences which must follow if they broke into the house – by these means and the probable idea that there were some arms in the house, time was given and two of the gentlemen made their escape and sent expressly for military aid. During this period I was induced by the most solemn assurances of the priest to go out at the back door to speak to six of the mob which six had been selected by Fr Ford and were said by him to have given up their arms. The object aimed at by my going out was to explain to the mob Mr Fox's views and by that means to pacify them and so assured by Fr Ford the other gentlemen permitted me to go out (they having previously pulled me back whenever I attempted to do so). The back door was then partly opened and I went out and attempted to speak but before one sentence could be delivered one of the six sprang forward and seized hold of me by the left breast with both hands and with all his force endeavoured to drag me amongst his companions. I was instantly dragged back into the house by those behind me and the door forcibly shut. Fr Ford's hat was knocked off in the scuffle when attempting to get between the six persons and myself.

After this a most furious attempt was made to force open both the back door and front door and also one of the windows, which window including glass and frame was broken. And the doors were only kept shut by the force and weight of the gentlemen and tenants inside who exerted themselves for my protection to the very utmost.

In this state we continued for several hours, the mob making constant and furious attacks to force the doors. I was again induced by the priests to speak to the mob through one of the broken windows when Fr Mc Gauran and some of the tenants placed themselves between the mob and myself with a view to prevent them firing at me. I then attempted to explain to them Mr Fox's views and with which they seemed in some degree pacified and soon after they got intelligence that the military were approaching and retired in regular order as they came.

They seemed well organised and under regular command.

D. Stewart.

A notice offering a reward for information refers to them as, 'totally unconnected with this neighbourhood and with Mr Fox's property'. Many of the tenants subscribed to the reward of £80. David Stewart does not specify 'the arrangements' which sparked the incident.

There may be a clue to the reason for this attack on the Lodge in a letter from Joshua Kells two years later, when he reported on a speech made by a Mr Kickham in Killinumerry:

He addressed his hearers on Sunday at great length as to Mr Stewart's arrangements … he stated that it was Mr Stewart's object to divest the Roman Catholics of their holdings and to replace them with Protestants and the works he said that were carrying on by Mr Stewart were no doubt great works but that the present generation would derive no benefit from them. He then compared Mr Stewart to the Roman Emperors.

Kells adds, 'We must not be governed by the arch Agitator O'Connell.'

Whatever the exaggerations of the speech, it was based on genuine fears of the Catholic tenantry. There were many Protestants on the estate and obviously the suggestion of twenty-five-year leases was a cause for anxiety. That same year Joshua Kells wrote to his brother, 'No arrangements has yet been made with any of the tenants ... Mr Armstrong was at the Lodge the other day and Mr Shanley, and John Stewart were sent for to meet him to consult together as to the propriety of giving leases to Protestant tenants exclusively.' He went on to advise against the wisdom of this.

Some months later David Stewart wrote a letter to Mr Fox about tenants and their leases. In it he stated that:

> ...matters will go from bad to worse if you and the other noblemen and Gentlemen of the Kingdom do not put a stop to the present flood of democracy and treason which pervade the lower classes ... nothing but anarchy and open rebellion can be the result ... [he asks] for the utmost exertion on the part of the landed proprietors and their agents to support them in the Conservative principles, with King, Lords, people each in their proper places. I should advise you not granting leases until your estates were properly arranged.

The defiance of the forty-shilling freeholders and granting of Catholic Emancipation was a shock still being absorbed.

The idea of people in their proper places was reiterated just a few years later and less than ten miles away, when Cecil T. Alexander penned the lines for a new hymn at Markree Castle, Co. Sligo:

> All things bright and beautiful,
> All creatures great and small,
> All things wise and wonderful,
> The Lord God made them all.
>
> The rich man in his castle,
> The poor man at his gate,
> He made them high or lowly,
> And ordered their estate.

Whatever the problems a ruined Bramham Park and mounting per-

Markree Castle. (*Photograph: Tommy Weir*)

sonal debts presented at home in Yorkshire, there is no hint of them in the landlordship of the Irish estates. George Lane-Fox, the Gambler, remained the benign landlord with a sense of duty to his tenants and great interest in the developments on the estate. Rents at this time amounted to approximately £3,000 a year from the Dromahaire estate. Duty dictated that a proportion of that revenue was reinvested in the estate. The programme of road-building and tree-planting continued apace. He paid frequent visits to Dromahaire and evidently enjoyed holidays there with his family. One letter from his agent Shanley reads, 'I presume the Misses Fox will soon return for the vacation which will gratify Mr Fox who is the fondest parent I ever saw.' There is evidence of a kindly nature almost to the extent of being a soft touch. When a Dr Johnson of Moydow Rectory, Co. Longford died, leaving a widow and five children, he wrote to Revd Armstrong:

> I have been anxiously considering the best means of alleviating their present distress. I should give up all arrears for the benefit of the children … I should pay for the benefit of the children for the next seven years the

difference between the rent which Dr Johnson would have paid and the rent for which I shall rent the lands. For house and land I should pay £25 a year for ten years and I will send someone over to make every arrangement for the situation of the orphans. I hope the poor little girls are better and I beg that you will be kind enough to remember me to them and to Mrs Armstrong.

His concern moved the Revd Armstrong to exclaim in a letter, 'I never knew a man of a more benevolent mind or of a more unwearied exertion to benefit the temporal and eternal condition of his fellow creatures.'

But no amount of goodwill and good intentions could alter the pattern of landholding and poor farming practices at work in Co. Leitrim in the period preceding the disaster of the Great Famine of 1845. However much George Lane-Fox was opposed to the subdivision of holdings, the practice continued in the face of the rapidly rising population. In Connaught, 64 per cent of farms were smaller than five acres by the 1840s. Farmers broke up their farms into small plots; an acre was sufficient to feed a family of five if planted with potatoes. There were 27,192 families living in Leitrim in 1841. Over 9,000 of them had holdings ranging from one to five acres and almost 8,000 had holdings of between five and fifteen acres. Just under 50 per cent of people lived in mud cabins having only one room described as, 'wretched buildings with some built of clay, mortar or bog-sods … contained little in the way of furniture – maybe a pot, shelf and small table'.

These stark statistics show the grinding poverty of the majority of the people living in Leitrim in the years preceding the famine. A letter from Joshua Kells to his brother at Bramham Park gives a picture of the poverty evident in Dromahaire. The letter dated 18 June 1834 is his annoyed response to an anonymous letter sent to George Lane-Fox. He writes:

It is stated that I am forming a road from the Bridge to the Pound House and destroying the potato gardens on the greatest part of the road in question.

The whole of it prior to Mr Stewart's departure was marked out on both sides – since then the Ditches have been made through a small field behind Carty the Smith about 12 perches but there was not a single potato destroyed for they did not plant them on the lie of the road. I stopped the work there after the small ditches were finished until the hay was cut in the Castle Park to prevent the possibility of any damage to the crops.

The next part you allude to is the decorating of the cottages outside (not forgetting the poverty within). All the outside work, mainly white-washing the cottages, was done by Mr Boland, the Magistrate, when the cholera broke out during the time we were in Waterford. After my return to Dromahaire there was not a brush laid on them. Mr Boland thought the whitewashing would stop the progress of the disease. With regard to the 'poverty within' you will admit there are three or four families living in sheds worse than pigstys where two or three sticks are put up against a wall with a little straw over and when the people are within the shed the hole is stopped up with straw when they enter to keep the storm out. Those and the persons that have got divisions in the Shriff Bog, it has been drained, and in the course of one year will produce as good crops as any part of the Manor of Dromahaire and enable the people to live comfortably...

An official report at this time paints a gloomy picture of the general standard of farming in the area:

The very idea of a rotation of crops is generally unknown and hardly any of the farmers have even the remotest notion either that a greater quantity might be raised by a proper variation of crops or that alteration of artificial pasture and tillage will allow this.

However by 1838 the Dromahaire Agricultural Society had been set up under the patronage of George Lane-Fox, with the aim of effecting change in farming practices. By this date the village was taking shape and now possessed a mill, a market-house, a dispensary, and schools in Drumlease and surrounding townlands catering for hundreds of children. The following report, sent by Mr E.H. Allingham secretary of the Society to the Chairman of the tenants on the Dromahaire Estate, outlines the efforts made to improve agriculture:

Next object of this society and its patron (George Lane-Fox) was to improve the system of agriculture in a country where it had hitherto been adopted in a most injudicious manner ... he has sent a gentleman of practical knowledge on agricultural and scientific pursuits to direct and encourage your endeavours ... very generally admitted by all the

The mill, Dromahaire. (*Photograph: Tommy Weir*)

most enlightened people in the name of Agriculture that the rotation system and horse feeding on green crops is the most effective method of correcting the baneful practices of farming already alluded to.

The report mentions the advantage of a fair-green, free of tolls and customs, which should encourage large numbers, but adds that a competition for turnip and red clover only attracted six competitors. The competition for turnip is significant as many landlords were already viewing the overdependence of the poorer tenants on the potato as a cause for concern. But the tone of the report is optimistic and continues:

Another great improvement has taken place, like the others at the sole expense of your landlord. I allude to the planting of both Forest Trees and White Thorn – some thousands of the former have been planted and I may safely say millions of the latter – all of which are doing well and already beginning to change the aspect of the country hitherto in a state of greater nudity of trees. This improvement is to be continued to a very great extent, if I may be allowed to conjecture so from the establishment of a nursery on an extension scale where the

136

tenant can be supplied with Trees – an inducement to encourage the planting of them. Your landlord has directed the ground to be planted by any tenant to be measured and be rent-free under certain restrictions such as keeping cattle of all sorts out of the plantation and not allowing any hock to be cut.

1. By the thinnings of the plantation the tenant will be supplied with timber suited for the erection of Dwelling-House, Stables and Cow sheds which latter many are without for lack of timber as other material [such as] stones are in great abundance.
2. By the growth of White-Thorn and other trees you have proper fences which all of you will admit is of greatest need – a source of litigation amongst neighbours.

The Dromahaire Dispensary has also undergone considerable alterations such as I think cannot fail to give satisfaction to each of you, as by these alterations the tenants paying under £5 rent are to be supplied with attendants and medicines free of any charge. From £5 upwards the scale of charges for attendance has been made in a ratio to the circumstances of the tenant ranging from 3 shillings a visit to 7 shillings, which is the maximum charge for a visit to any tenant.

There was a sense of optimism and progress when William Kernaghan set up steam navigation on Lough Gill in the early 1840s. Merchants from Sligo travelled on the boat *The Lady of the Lake* to the butter-market in Dromahaire which had been established by George Lane-Fox's agent Joshua Kells in 1845. There was much talk of the proposed canal which would link Lough Allen and Lough Gill to support timber and grain industry. Plans were also afoot for a railway line between the two lakes, which would pass through the Lane-Fox estates. The railway line and William Kernaghan's efforts to secure the lease for the mill at Dromahaire were the issues most discussed in the correspondence between Dromahaire and Bramham Park in the years immediately preceding and during the catastrophic famine, which struck in 1845.

George Lane-Fox continued to be the benevolent landlord through the 1830s and '40s. He particularly valued education and established an extraordinary number of schools throughout his estate catering for hundreds of children. In a letter to David Stewart in June 1843 he admitted,

'I could not afford any further outlay of money on my Irish properties.'
Two years later when there was a request for a school in Killanummery.
David Stewart urged caution and his letter illustrates some of the
expenditure on schools:

From David Stewart to Thomas Kells 29th April 1845

Mr Fox has already built an excellent schoolhouse at Dromahaire at an
expense of several hundred pounds and placed the school under the auspices of Revd Wynne, besides building the schoolhouse Mr Fox allows
£15 per annum to the Schoolmaster, a very large garden and a cow's graze.
The school is very well attended generally. Mr Fox has also established
eleven or twelve schools by giving houses, good gardens and various sums
of money to each school. These schools are all under auspices of several
clergymen of the Established Church and should any other school be necessary it will be easy for Mr Fox to establish an additional one. Children
of all denominations are taught indiscriminately in each of these schools
and some of the teachers are Roman Catholic but the Scriptures are read
in all of them. I consider that schools so stable and so conducted are more
useful to the children of the tenants and the children of the labourers than
any National School can be under present circumstances and so long as

Protestant school, Dromahaire. (*Photograph: Tommy Weir*)

the Scriptures are not allowed to be read in the National Schools, which is the case at present.'

He advises great caution 'in answering the prayer of the petitioner'. But George Lane-Fox found it hard to say no and a second letter followed on the very next day:

> Mr Fox states that he has already expended considerable sums of money in building and repairing Schoolhouses and paying Schoolmasters and Schoolmistresses on the different parts of his estate but if it can be proved that an additional schoolhouse is necessary he will build one at his own expense and without drawing on the public purse and that he considered it desirable that the children should have the power to read the Scripture in all schools and that such schools be inspected and examined by the clergymen of the respective parishes.

The letters also show his commitment to the Protestant ethic of reading the bible, which was not done in the new National Schools being set up to cater for Catholic children.

In a report on his Irish estates it was claimed that the arrears due on the Dromahaire estate to 1 May 1844 amounted to £4,907 12s 4d. The report went on to propose that the whole of the arrears should be given up as there was 'no possibility of recovery'. Instead the tenants should be given leases of twenty-one years, 'an inducement to manage their farms well'. About 500 tenants would be involved. There was a recommendation that the land immediately around the town of Dromahaire leading to the river mouth, including Stone Park and Stone Park Mountain, should not be on a farm lease but should be reserved for building purposes.

Two years before the famine struck, George Lane-Fox was clearly delighted by an address of appreciation forwarded to him by his Dromahaire tenants. In reply he wrote:

> During the whole course of my life nothing has given me greater sat-isfaction than the letter I have this day received from you enclosing an address from 128 of my tenants in the Manor of Dromahaire – the kind and affectionate sentiments expressed by them will be long felt by me as a proof that the good feeling which it has been my desire to establish

between my tenantry and myself and that the expense I have been at for their benefit has been well bestowed upon a grateful people. My sole object has been the comfort and happiness of the occupiers of the land...

It is clear that his benevolence was a cause of exasperation to his agent Joshua Kells for two weeks after that letter in June 1843 Joshua wrote to his brother Thomas at Bramham Park as follows:

Will you have the goodness to take the opportunity of receiving Mr Fox's directions as to how far he will continue to give provisions to a few poor families here who have been in the habit of receiving potatoes and meal at this season of the year. I am constantly tormented with them but will do nothing without Mr Fox's directions. If he wishes to give a little help for a time to the most needful and helpless families I will employ them in hay-making and other necessary jobs but it not be done to any great extent and the able-bodied labourers can seek for employment elsewhere which can be had at this season of the year. The villagers have cows on Mr Fox's grass and a shed is built which holds about 20 of them. Those cows are kept the whole year round by Mr Fox. Therefore we should have to employ haymakers for this purpose in the summer season. There are 50 cows on the grass about Dromahaire and the rent is paid by the butter and the milk is a great help to support the poor families. Under these circumstances you will have an idea how the matter stands.

David Stewart in exactly the same month of June was writing from Waterford in the same vein:

Mr Fox took the payment of the Tithes upon himself and up to this hour has never charged any Irish tenant one shilling additional rent. Mr Fox's plan of his estate and mine then and wherever I have been employed, has been to go in quietly and without puffing like some others, but I will venture to say that there are not many landlords in Ireland that have been more liberal to their tenants or who have done more to improve their estates and the condition of the tenantry than Mr Fox ... [he is] in the first ranks of the very best Landlords in the Three Kingdoms.

The payment of tithes for the support of the Protestant Church was

Protestant church, Dromahaire (*Photograph: Tommy Weir*).

a matter of great resentment for the Catholic population. In the Tithe Rent Charge Act of 1838, the tithe payments had been incorporated into the rental charge, which laid the responsibility for collection on the landlords, but they were able to pass the tithe amount on to their tenants. Obviously George Lane-Fox had not done this, a gesture that would be appreciated by his largely Catholic tenantry.

There was a lot of misery and poverty on the estate and tenants could lodge personal petitions directly to the landlord for relief. But not all were lucky, as the following petition from one Henry McLoughlin shows:

> Petition of Henry McLoughlin late a tenant on your Honour's estate in Dromahaire;
> Most humbly I herewith state that Petitioner now upwards of 80 years of age is from a variety of circumstances reduced to the most abject state of want and destitution, dependent solely on the support on the very limited means of his son-in-law who has a wife and three helpless children whom he is barely able to support.
> That your honour's Petitioner upwards of five years back was ejected

for non payment of rent and arrears from the lands of Clerand near Dromshanbo where petitioner and his ancestors lived for more than 200 years solvent and improving tenants by whom a shilling was never lost by any landlord ... That poor Petitioner humbly prays that his distressed state will be taken into your Honour's humane and merciful consideration ... and humbly prays that some provision such as your honour granted to other aged and distressed tenants – those whom Petitioner hopes he will not be deemed less worth, or a small house with a few acres of land to afford common necessities during the few years that Petitioner has in all probability to live which will enable Poor Petitioner to die in peace to bless your Honour as Bountiful ... For whom he will ever pray.

Joshua Kells forwarded the petition accompanied by a letter, chilling in its practicality, to his brother at Bramham in November 1844:

Perhaps you will be good enough to lay the enclosed before Mr Fox at his convenience. Henry Mc Loughlin has forwarded it to me. At the time he was ejected he owed Mr Fox an arrear of £237. 5. 8. His son was a profligate and was the cause of the old man's ruin – he is now in Australia. The old man is in distress. A matter of £5 or £10 would be of much use to him, and land, he is not capable of managing it, and he is too feeble to work, in short, he cannot long survive. We have the weather very wild at present. I am sorry to say there is a serious shortage ... many have lost three quarters of the crop. The price is good for oats, butter and pigs. I trust therefore to have the rents.

An occasional tenant made a direct approach to the landlord. In May 1846, one brave soul, Catherine Dolan, journeyed over in person to Bramham Park to plead her case, in a dispute with her brother over the family home, which had been lost over arrears of rent. She enlisted the help of a local clergyman, Revd Fisher, as an intermediary. Her temerity caused great consternation. George Lane-Fox was annoyed at Revd Fisher's interference. Back in Dromahaire Joshua Kells wrote to his brother, 'Is it not wonderful the lengths to which those people will go to make their case?' The Revd Mc Keon, similarly outraged, wrote to Joshua Kells referring to Revd Fisher, 'I hope in future he will not take up every trifling case.' Poor Catherine Dolan.

David Stewart, in particular, was strongly protective of his employer's

Famine scene.

Famine Soup Pot,
Office of Public
Works, Dromahaire.
(*Photograph: Tommy
Weir*)

interests, to the extent of being highly suspicious of William Kernaghan's efforts to secure the lease on the Mill at Dromahaire. The terms of the lease were debated backwards and forwards in an extraordinary way. In one period alone between September and November 1845 there were fifteen letters exchanged between Stewart and Kernaghan and a further fourteen between Stewart and Joshua Kells at Bramham. His fear that Lane-Fox was being duped by a wily business man is clear. Sometime during the summer of 1844, William Kernaghan had gone over to Yorkshire to see George Lane-Fox in person. They had evidently hit it off, for Joshua Kells wrote from Dromahaire in September:

> I have seen Mr Kernaghan since his return from Bramham and he is much pleased with his interview with Mr Fox. I submit that his lease should be given a number of years (say 99) without a valuation clause. Mr Kernaghan has done a good deal for the benefit of Mr Fox's property, the Mills are very substantial and extensive, he is therefore deserving of a fair lease.

He refers for the first time to Mr Fox's illness, 'I sincerely hope Mr Fox is now well, I am sorry to hear he was complaining.' He casually adds a P.S. which, on the eve of the famine, has a certain resonance, 'All is going well here, the weather is favourable and the crops in good order.' The agreement was drawn up in early December 1844:

> I hereby propose to take from George Lane-Fox that Plot of Ground called the New Mill Site situate in the town of Dromahaire in the Co. of Leitrim bounded on the one side by the River Bonet ... and at the one end by the present Mill Plot called Hozey's Plot and at the other end by a line drawn fifty feet from the Pound Wall leading to the River Bonet with an exclusive right of a Mill at the yearly rent of – per annum payable quarterly from 1st May next for 65 years with a right of renewal of 21 more at a cheaper rent...

The rental would prove to be a sticking point, with David Stewart suggesting £25 and Kernaghan offering £10. In the ensuing flurry of letters Stewart's outrage shows; he appears convinced that Kernaghan was not stating the facts clearly. Some samples show both the clash of interests and personality of the two men. Stewart writes:

> Mr Kernaghan has taken special care in his correspondence with
> Mr Fox not to mention the Mill Plot and the site of his own cottage
> nor the Miller's cottage built by Mr Fox but has confined himself to the
> Agreement about the Mill Race, the rent of which was not to exceed
> £20 nor to be below £10, by this means he has induced Mr Fox to
> fix his rent at just the one half of the lowest sum at which it should be
> fixed. Of course if Mr Fox were to make Mr Kernaghan a present of
> the whole I should have no right to object but I cannot help observing
> that Mr Kernaghan's conduct in attempting to the utmost of his power
> from first to last to impose upon Mr Fox and everyone employed by
> him cannot fairly entitle him to any favour ... [there] cannot be just
> reason for showing favour to a person who persists in such a system of
> duplicity.

His persistence succeeded in holding up the signing of the lease and
Kernaghan wrote to Mr Fox in January 1845:

> Dear Sir, Beggars can't be choosers, consequently I am obliged to yield
> to this fact of very great Injustice. You, I don't blame, not knowing our
> agreements but I do Mr Stewart, who knows as well as I did the spirit and
> intention of the agreement. Please direct your Law Agents to forward me
> drafts of the leases for the approval by my solicitor ... In this so unpleasant
> transaction between tenant and Landlord I would say personally I beg to
> express my thanks. If you can come to Dromahaire I hope you will, you
> may be able to judge whether D. Stewart or I am right.

By March 1845 matters had not been settled, as Kernaghan colourfully
put it in a letter, 'The ides of March and no lease yet.' All through the
dispute George Lane-Fox remained ill, adding further to David Stewart's
annoyance and anxiety. He wrote, 'I hope most sincerely that Mr Fox is
quite well.' By August he was 'thankful to God that Mr Fox is better' and
remarks that 'Mr Kernaghan's troubling Mr Fox is very bad.' Meanwhile
Kernaghan was blaming 'Mr Stewart's duplicity as well as my own sim-
plicity'. It was time for the Kells brothers to intervene. In a letter in July
1845 he said:

I am sure that Mr Fox is anxious that the business should be brought to a close. You will be very sorry to hear that Mr Fox has been unwell for sometime. I am however happy to say that he is a little better and I hope in a short time he will be well.

He also wrote to his brother at Bramham about Kernaghan, 'it is unpleasant his affairs not having been settled sooner, he only blames Mr Stewart not himself' and confided that Mr Fox had been in favour of Kernaghan all along. One suspects that Kernaghan was possibly getting a good deal and that George Lane-Fox, who was in very poor health, was anxious to have the matter settled. Eventually, the lease was agreed. The details are irrelevant, for as they were being decided, famine was devastating Leitrim. The grim irony was that within a short time span of three years, all the large mills were lying idle.

★ ★ ★ ★ ★

It has been estimated that the potato blight, which spread through

George Lane-Fox, 'The Squire'. (*Courtesy of Nicholas Lane-Fox*)

Ireland in 1845, destroyed one third of the crop. The percentage in parts of Leitrim was much higher, with three quarters of potatoes lost in the region around Manorhamilton, while in Dromahaire many of the potatoes were found to be 'utterly unfit for use'. The over dependence of a huge population on a single crop was to have dire consequences.

The mortality rate of Black '47, the worst year of the famine, shows Leitrim with the fourth highest death rate of the whole country, with a figure of 3.9 per cent of population. This corresponds to an approximately 60,000 deaths. Death was due to starvation and to the spread of diseases such as dysentery and typhus, as the workhouses at Manorhamilton and Carrick-on-Shannon became overcrowded. It was a tragedy on a massive scale. Harrowing scenes of a starving people must have been in evidence everywhere especially in the poor sod cabins of Leitrim. One description in 1847 reads, 'In some instances, particularly in Leitrim, whole families are discovered to be dead in their cabins by the stench that proceeds from their putrid bodies. The dead are frequently buried in bogs, cabbage plots and even in the houses where they died.' It became a common practice to pull down the thatched roof of the cabin to form a mass grave.

The infamous Gregory Clause of the Poor Law made it impossible for anyone with a quarter of an acre to enter the workhouse. This led to countless starving people giving up their small parcels of land in order to gain relief. This, coupled with the fact that the Poor Law made landlords responsible for paying poor rates on all holdings valued at £4 or less, became an enticement for landlords to clear their estates of the small tenants and to consolidate their farms. Indeed many members of the Government in London, such as Lord Palmerstown and Lord Clanricarde, were of the opinion that any improvement in the social system in Ireland was dependent on the ejectment of small holders and of squatting cottiers.

There was a mixed reaction from landlords. The Earl of Lucan cleared 2,000 people in Mayo between 1846 and 1849. The Marquis of Sligo, also in Mayo, evicted many of his tenants, some of them illegally. In Roscommon, Major Denis Mahon cleared his estates of 605 families, having given them a choice of eviction or assisted passage to Canada. Many of those who chose to emigrate perished when one of the notorious 'coffin ships' sank *en route* to Canada. The medical officer at Quebec reported that the survivors were the 'most wretched and diseased he had ever seen'. When news of the sinking reached Roscommon, distraught relatives attacked and murdered Major Denis Mahon in November 1847.

In contrast, Sir Robert Gore-Booth of Lissadell in Co. Sligo spent £35,000 of his own money on importing and distributing food between August 1846 and July 1847. He dispensed 140 gallons of soup and 150 loaves of bread a day and sold 30 tons of Indian meal per week. Nobody was forcibly evicted and he made a request for land in Canada to place tenants, and with careful preparations 1,000 tenants were sent to Canada. Other benevolent landlords were Edward Cooper of Markree Castle in Sligo, Alexander Percival of Templehouse and John Wynne of Hazelwood. In Leitrim, Charles Manners St George, though an absentee, showed concern for his tenants through his agent Charles Cox. The same was true on the Dromahaire estate of George Lane-Fox. In 1843, two years before the famine, David Stewart, wrote another letter showing his management of the estate. He says that Mr Fox:

> ...by his own spontaneous act, has invariably let his land tithe free both in England and Ireland, but in Ireland he took the payment of tithes upon himself and up until this time has never charged any Irish tenant one shilling additional rent, long before the Government interfered in the business. The abolition of Tolls, the formation of scores of miles of roads, the making of hundreds of miles of drains, the supporting of all the widows on his estate, the support of the poor up to this time without allowing any one of them to receive any reliance from the parish or from the workhouse and innumerable beneficial acts ... the certainty of his conduct has proved himself to be (if not the very best) amongst the land-lords in existence in either Ireland or any other country.

George Lane-Fox was in poor health during the famine years and died in 1848 just as the famine was ending. He had been appointed High Sheriff of Leitrim a year previously, an honour many must have felt was his due. During the famine his agent, Joshua Kells, became an active member of the Relief Committee in Dromahaire set up to organise the distribution of food in the area and to supervise and facilitate the aid provided by the Quakers, which was so important when there was a halt to the public works in early 1847. He was also on the Relief Committee of Killanummery and that of Killarga and Cloonlougher, representing some of the townlands of the Lane-Fox estate. He was therefore in a position to write a letter to the *Manchester Guardian* in May 1848 replying to an article entitled, 'Distressing Case – An evicted Irish Family'. In the letter, he states that as agent to George Lane-Fox, he is replying to the article:

> ...in which it is stated that Patrick Gallagher and his family are in such destitution near Manchester having been lately dislodged from the estate of a Mr Fox in Co. Leitrim. As I know no other proprietor of this name in this county I beg to deny the charge against Mr Fox for his having dislodged Patrick Gallagher and his large family of eleven children. Mr Fox has lately arranged with his numerous Tenantry without a single case of eviction up to this date and he has also given direction to employ and provide for the poor on his estate in time of Scarcity.

David Stewart wrote an account in 1846, giving a sober assessment of the estate as the Famine entered its second year. It sums up the situation for most landlords, with their tenantry in dire straits. The landlords were finding it impossible to get their rents and were also having to foot the bill for the famine relief under New Poor Law. Many of them found it difficult and were less able to continue their philanthropic role. There is also in the report, a sense of his feelings of the inadequacy of the help on offer and his uncertainty in the face of a disaster of such proportion. He refers to the 'present unhappy circumstance of the country and the great fall in the price of farm produce'. He continues:

> I must now observe that there are very considerable numbers of tenants upon this estate, whose holdings or farms as they are called are so small and the lands so poor and who at the same time have such large families of small children, that they cannot pay any rent and even keep their families from starving without assistance from their Landlord or from the Poor Rates. These men, generally but not always, are very willing to work if they can get work to do. Before the Poor Law was established and up to this time, Mr Fox supported all such persons upon his Estate (with scarcely an exception) either by giving them work by the piece or employing them by the day but generally employing them at task work. Besides the above class of tenants there are upon this estate many widows, most of them with large families, utterly incapable of supporting themselves and their families without assistance. To all such, Mr Fox has hitherto given assistance by

employing themselves at such work as they could do and when at times they could not do any work due to ill-health, they have been assisted to oatmeal or potatoes by Mr Fox. In fact all the poor on both estates have been supported by Mr Fox up to the time of the New Poor Law being established and now that the Landlord's share of the new poor rate will be much heavier and more expensive than the relief formerly given to the poor by Mr Fox and yet the poor people not so well taken care of. I should therefore submit that all such poor Tenants as cannot pay the whole of their rents in money should be allowed to pay such parts of their rents in labour as they cannot pay in money – such labour to be done in draining or making fences by the piece under directions ... They cannot pay their rents in money and in the present state of Ireland no Landlord can safely turn away such tenants. Besides the above description of tenants there are at present upwards of two hundred young men on the Dromahaire Estate who have no land and if these young men are allowed to marry and bring their wives and families into their Father's, Mother's or Brother's houses they will divide and sub-divide the farms into such small patches, as will in the end and speedily too render it impossible for the land to support the people, even without paying rent. I would therefore submit that such of those young men as cannot be settled upon the newly reclaimed land should be assisted to emigrate to Canada or some other country. If they remain at home it will be found next to impossible to prevent their dividing the farm. By this letter you will see very clearly my views of the present state of Ireland and also my views as to the best plan for Mr Fox to adopt under the present embarrassing circumstances.

D. Stewart.

Relief measures in Leitrim were undertaken by Boards of Guardians and Relief Committees who organised the workhouses and distribution of food. Joshua Kells served on the Dromahaire Committee in company with Captain Palmer of Shriff, Whyte of Newtown Manor and Hugh Gillmor. There was an increase in the number of paupers in the Dromahaire area and the Quakers reported 'scenes of poverty and wretchedness beyond belief'. The spread of fever led to temporary fever hospitals being set up both in Dromahaire and Drumkeerin. There were just a few instances of assisted passage to Canada; in 1846, £88 covered the cost of twenty emigrants to Canada and there was a request

Nicholas and Rachel Lane-Fox and family. (*Courtesy of Nicholas Lane-Fox*)

to the Poor Law Commissioners for permission for ninety to emigrate in 1849. Emigration increased, but at people's own expense, and very often with help and remittances sent by those who had gone earlier.

It is an understatement to say that all relief measures, whether by way of Public Works set up to employ people, workhouse, soup kitchens and most especially by the meagre measures given by a grudging government policy which did not want to interfere with trade, were all grossly inadequate. In the ten years between 1841 and 1851 the population of Leitrim declined by 43,382, far more than its present population of 28,000. The majority had died from starvation and disease and the remainder had emigrated. Again it is difficult to visualize these numbers in the quiet countryside of today's Leitrim. In David Thomson's *Woodbrook* he wrote about an area near Carrick-on-Shannon. He describes the moment when he realised the significance of the names they so casually called the fields around them – Flanagan's Rock, Clancy's Rock, Meehan's garden, Martin's garden, M'Lannie's, Higgin's Cresswell's, Conlon's, Cregan's, Luggy's. Whole families had lived there, the houses had been pulled down and just fragments of the stone walls remained.

★ ★ ★ ★ ★

The Great Famine of 1845-1848 was a catalyst for change in Ireland's history. This was especially true in the relationship between landlord and tenant. George Lane-Fox's death in 1848, just as the famine ended, marked the beginning of the demise of the all-powerful landlord. The landlord classes had been members of Parliament, justices of the peace, Poor Law guardians, managers and patrons of schools. Their position diminished through the second half of the nineteenth century. As early as 1836 the new constabulary took matters of law from their control. Agrarian crime increased after the famine and there was a demand from the tenants for the 3 f's: Fair Rent, Fixity of Tenure and Free Sale. The old policy of letting land on a yearly basis, with the possibility of a rent increase, and if evicted, no right to compensation for improvements, had for long been a matter of contention. When Gladstone became Prime Minister he had famously stated that 'my mission is to pacify Ireland'. In 1869 he disestablished the Church of Ireland, which settled the matter of the tithes. In the face of agrarian outrages, he became committed to settling the Land Question. The horror of the famine had entered the Irish psyche and the whole question of the nature of landholding would surface as the century progressed. With the passage of the Land Act of 1870, tenants achieved some rights regarding their holdings. Now, they could only be evicted for non-payment of rent and were entitled to compensation for improvements if they surrendered their leases but they still had not been granted fixity of tenure. There was a depression in the 1870s and evictions for non-payment mounted. This resulted in continuing outrages and in 1879 Michael Davitt founded the Land League to redress the grievances of the tenants. He was later joined by Parnell who was committed to the idea of Home Rule for Ireland. It was a powerful combination that fired the nation's aspirations.

George Lane-Fox, 'The Squire', who took over the landlordship after his father's death in 1848 until his own death in 1896, experienced this period of profound change. On the surface some things remained the same. He and his family continued to visit the estate on holiday and to oversee the work of his agents Joshua Kells and later Francis La Touche. An excellent horseman, he hunted with the local gentry; the Whites of Fivemilebourne, the Palmers of Shriff and the Wynnes of Hazlewood. In England he was one of the finest amateur coachmen and his coach is now on display in the Castle Museum in York. He also brought back the famous Bramham hounds from Harewood where they had been since his grandfather's death. Obviously George Lane-Fox, 'the Gambler', had not been a keen huntsman. On his visits to Ireland the Squire enjoyed making contact with the Irish Master of Hounds to compare and contrast the various breeds. Irish hounds had always been highly regarded in England, from the Irish Wolfhound to foxhound, and today Irish stallion hounds are routinely used by packs in England. When the Squire inherited he was left with his father's gambling debts of £175,000. He took the task of settling these debts very seriously. As a result he was never able to afford to rebuild Bramham Park. In Ireland he remained a popular landlord and on one of his visits to Dromahaire in 1875, he was greeted by cheering crowds and blazing bonfires.

The formation of the Land League excited thousands of tenant farmers throughout Ireland and expectations rose. At a meeting in Drumkeerin in July 1880, which attracted over 8,000 people from the surrounding countryside, the secretary of the Land League, Thomas McGivney, stated that no legislation on the Irish land question could be satisfactory or permanent, 'which does not abolish the present system of landlordism and establish in its stead a peasant proprietorship'.

A few months later there was a huge rally in Dromahaire. Like Drumkeerin there was a carnival atmosphere with marching bands and the crowd wore green scarves and ribbons. The local clergy were there in support. Francis La Touche, who was land agent for a number of landlords, was denounced for the eviction of a Mr O'Rourke. Those who took land from an evicted tenant were condemned as land-grabbers.

From the 1850s, rising agricultural prices due to the Crimean War had resulted in growing numbers of strong farmers, merchants and shopkeepers. The paternalistic role of the landlord was on the wane, and equally, so was the subservient one of the tenant. During the Land War of 1879-1882 it became popular to demonise the landlord class. Even Gore-Booth was attacked for sending his tenants to Canada.

While indeed some landlords had seen emigration as a way of clearing their estates, others like Gore-Booth had done it for philanthropic reasons. Desperate people had viewed it as an escape from the workhouse and death. These rallies in Leitrim were just two years after the assassination of William Sydney Clements, 3rd Earl of Leitrim. He resided on the Lough Rynn Estate with vast lands in Leitrim, Donegal, Sligo and Roscommon. He was notorious for his harsh treatment of tenants and pitiless eviction policy. He was certainly a strange man. Among many complaints, he had on occasion ordered the shooting of the goats of the poor because they were damaging his trees. He sacked his blacksmith because he had allowed the tenants, who were waiting in a cold courtyard to pay their rents, to warm themselves at the forge fire. He was disliked by the other Irish MPs in Parliament and became isolated when he falsified reports of agrarian crime on his estate. There were two attempts on his life and he was forced to travel with an armed escort. In 1878, there were many evictions pending in Donegal when he set out to go to his house in Milford in the county. Impatiently he did not wait for his escort but he had two loaded revolvers. He was attacked and killed by three men at Cratlagh Wood near Milford. His driver and clerk were also killed. At his funeral in Dublin, the cortège was attacked by angry onlookers as it made its way to the family vault in St Michan's church. Despite a large reward for information his killers were never found.

Of course the reality for many landlords was that rents had remained almost unchanged since the 1840s. Many had low levels of rent returns and some landlords were suffering from mounting debts. The passage of the 1881 Land Act gave the tenants the right to seek reductions in their rents and some security of tenure. But many tenants now aspired to ownership of their land and a few years later the Ashbourne Act of 1885 facilitated land purchase.

Landlords continued to play a role as leaders in society and were committed to community affairs. Railway fever was gripping the country and George Lane-Fox was involved with the construction of the Sligo, Leitrim and Northern Railway. He and Robert Gore-Booth of Lissadell became investors in the railway. The railway line ran through much of his land on its journey from Sligo to Enniskillen and opened in 1879. It was of great value to the livestock trade – cattle being transported from Enniskillen for export to England via Derry or Belfast. He was business-like in his dealings, leaving most of his correspondence to solicitors and stewards, whether in the matter of the railway or purchasing trees from the Wynnes of Hazelwood. As a staunch Protestant, he initially refused to grant a site for a Catholic church in Dromahaire. Mass was celebrated in various houses in the area. The nearest church was in Newtownmanor, built in 1825 on a site presented by John Whyte, a Catholic landowner. But George Lane-Fox had a change of heart when his son George Frederick converted to Catholicism on his marriage to Annette Weld-Blundell who was from an old English Catholic family. It meant that George Frederick would not inherit Bramham Park but a loving relationship with his father continued. In the 1880s, Francis La Touche gave the parish priest, Fr McSharry, the good news that a site on the east bank of the Bonet River had been granted by the landlord, rent free forever, for the erection of a Catholic church. In addition, George Lane-Fox gave a donation of £50 towards the construction of the church and his agent, Francis La Touche gave £20. The church of St Patrick opened in Dromahaire on 9 March 1890.

The erosion of the landlord's position and power continued under the advance of the Land League and Home Rule. The success of Parnell in the 1880 election gave the people a new focus of political power. Throughout the 1870s and 1880s there was a fostering of an Irish identity with a renewed interest in Irish culture such as the Irish language, dancing and music, which culminated in the founding of the Gaelic League in 1893 by Douglas Hyde. The Gaelic Athletic Association was set up in 1884 to encourage Irish games such as football and hurling. There was a strong sense of Irish Nationalism.

In the late 1800s, agriculture suffered a decline and as a result land began to cease to be a good investment. When the land legislation policies of the Government introduced the idea of land purchase schemes, it was an attractive proposition for some landlords as well as tenants. The Ashbourne Act of 1881 made £5 million available for land purchase and another Act followed in 1885. The tenant would repay the loan in an annuity. No doubt George Lane-Fox watched all these movements of change with great interest and with a growing realisation of what the future held for the landlord class.

George Lane-Fox, the Squire, died in 1896 and for a short time he was succeeded by his younger son James as his elder son George Frederick had renounced his claim when he became a Catholic. James was in ill-health and in a short time was succeeded by his son George Richard Lane-Fox in 1906. The Wyndam Act of 1903 had greatly facilitated land purchase, with £12 million made available. An added attraction for the tenant was that his annuity would be less than his rental payment. For the landlord it was certain money with an additional tempting offer of bonuses and shares. It was this Act that decisively made it easier for the tenants to purchase their lands and lessened landlord control. A further Act in 1909 introduced compulsory purchase in congested areas, whereby the landlord had no choice and had to sell his estates. By 1914, 9 million acres had been transferred from landlord to tenant with over 75 per cent of occupiers buying out their landlord. Amongst them, was the estate of Dromahaire of the Lane-Fox family, which passed to the Irish Land Commission.

The sale at least enabled George Richard Lane-Fox to take on the task of restoring Bramham Park. He set out to recreate, as closely as possible, Robert Benson's original design. He had a distinguished career. He was a Member of Parliament for Barkston Ash from 1906 to 1931, a Privy Councillor and Secretary of State for the mines in Stanley Baldwin's Government. He was created Lord Bingley in 1933.

The Lane-Fox family retained their link to Dromahaire for many years. In 1917 a Mrs Timoney received a touching letter on the death of her son James in the First World War. It was from the chaplain of 1st Battalion Irish Guards. His name was Fr Richard John Lane-Fox, son of George Frederick. In it he says:

> He was killed instantly by a shell and I buried him myself in a graveyard beside others of his regiment and he has over him a good cross with his name inscribed upon it ... I said Mass for him in the presence of his comrades who prayed for him when they went to Holy Communion...

He finished the letter with the words, 'I knew him well and I take a special interest in the men who come from my old home in Dromahaire.' It seems clear that the Lane-Fox family retained affectionate memories of the area.

Over in Yorkshire at the present time, the Lane-Fox family still reside at Bramham Park –direct descendants of Robert Benson, 1st Lord Bingley. The present owner is another George Lane-Fox. His son Nicholas, with his wife Rachel and their five children, continue the family tradition of running an estate in an efficient and progressive manner. The estate is a working farm growing a variety of crops and has a dairy herd, beef cattle and Jacob's sheep. They have a commitment to the environment, having two designated sites of special scientific interest which preserve wildlife habitats. A variety of events take place on the estate such as the Leeds Musical festival and in particular the famous three-day Bramham Horse Trials, an event that in recent years received an award for best British Equestrian event. The Lane-Fox family still continues in their role of contributing to the welfare and benefit of the community.

Today the ruins of O'Rourke's Banqueting Hall, Villiers Castle and the Lodge are clustered closely together at the entrance to the village of Dromahaire; symbols of three distinct stages in our history: that of the Chieftain, Planter and Landlord. The Banqueting Hall evokes the memory of the proud, independent chieftainship of the O'Rourkes who ruled Breifne for 700 years. Villiers Castle is tangible proof of the success of the Tudor and Stuart conquest with the arrival of the Planter. The Lodge became the home of the landlord and his agent, who were ultimately left with the responsibility of administering a large area of Breifne – a role and task that eventually became untenable in the rise of a country aspiring to independence.

List of Sources

Primary Sources

O'Donovan, J., (ed.) *Annals of the Four Masters* (Dublin, 1851).

Hennessy, (ed.) *Annals of Loch Ce* (London, 1871).

Calendar of State Papers, 1584–1604, 1615–1632.

Scott, A.B., & Martin, F.X. (eds) *Expugnatio Hibernica: The Conquest of Ireland by Giraldis Cambrensis* (Royal Irish Academy: Dublin, 1978).

Topographia, Giraldis Cambrensis.

Song of Dermot and the Earl Goddard Orpen (trans.) (Clarendon Press: Oxford, 1892).

Captain de Cuellar's Letter and Account of his stay in Ireland.

Depositions for South Leitrim, 1641, Trinity College Dublin Manuscript Department.

Lane Fox Papers, West Yorkshire Archives, National Library Dublin.

Secondary Sources

Canny, N., *Making Ireland British* (Oxford University Press: Oxford, 2001).

Chambers, A., *Chieftain to Knight* (New Island Books: Dublin, 1983).

Curtis, E., *A History of Medieval Ireland* (Ernest Benn Ltd: London, 1938).

Dunlevy, M., *Dress In Ireland* (Holmes and Meier: New York, 1989).

De Blacam, A., *The Great Retreat* (The Capuchin Annual 1946–7).

Edwards, D., *Ireland in the Age of the Tudors* (Barnes and Noble: London, 1977).

Hickson, M. A., *Ireland in the 17th Century* (London, 1884).

Jackson, A., *Ireland 1798-1998* (Blackwell Publishers: Oxford, 1999).

Kelly, L., *A Flame Now Quenched* (Lilliput Press: Dublin, 1998).

Kilfeather, T.P., *Graveyard of the Spanish Armada* (Anvil Books: Dublin, 1967).

Lockyer, R., *Buckingham, The Life and Political Career of George Villiers* (Longman Press: London, 1981).

Loeber, R., *A Biographical Dictionary of Architects of Ireland* (John Murray: London, 1981).

Loeber, R., 'A Gate to Connaught – The Building of Jamestown, Co. Leitrim' (*The Irish Sword*).

McGarry, P., 'My Lord of Lanesborough', *Rathcline* (Rathcline Heritage Society, 1995).

MacAtasney, G., *Leitrim and the Great Hunger* (Carrick-on-Shannon & District Historical Society: Carrick-on-Shannon, 1997).

Mc Dermott, B., *O'Ruairc of Breifne* (Drumlin Publications: Leitrim, 1990).

MacGallogly, D., 'Brian Oge and the Nine-Years'-War' (*Breifne*).

MacGallogly, D., 'Brian of the Ramparts O'Rourke 1566–1592' (*Breifne* 2 1962).

Moran, G., *Sir Robert Gore-Booth and his landed estate in Co. Sligo 1814-1876* (Four Courts Press: Dublin, 2006).

Morgan, H., 'Extradition and Treason – Trial of a Gaelic Lord – the case of Brian O'Rourke' (*Irish Jurist* 22, 1987).

Nicholls, K., *Gaelic and Gaelicised Ireland in the Middle Ages* (Gill & Macmillan: Dublin, 1972).

O'Dowd, M., *Power, Politics and Land in Early Modern Sligo 1568-1688* (Institute of Irish Studies: Belfast, 1981).

O'Duigneain, P., *North Leitrim in Famine Times and North Leitrim in Land League Times* (Drumlin Publications: Leitrim, 1986).

O'Duigneain, P., *Dromahaire: Story and Pictures* (Drumlin Publications: Leitrim, 1990).

Orpen, G. H., *Ireland under the Normans* (Four Courts Press: Dublin, 2005).

O'Sullivan Beare, P., M.J. Byrne (trans.) *Ireland under Elizabeth* (Catholic University Press: New York, 1970).

Porter, C., (ed.) *The Great Irish Famine* (Mercier Press: Cork, 1995).

Roche, R., *The Norman Invasion of Ireland* (Anvil Press: Dublin, 1998).

Thompson, D., *Woodbrook* (Vintage Publications, 1974).

Treadwell, V., *Buckingham and Ireland 1616-1628* (Four Courts Press: Dublin, 1998).

Vaughan, W.E., *Landlords and tenants in Ireland 1848-1904* (Economic and Social History Society of Ireland: Dublin, 1984).

Unpublished Theses

MacCuarta, B., *Newcomers to the Irish Midlands (1540–1641)* (M.A., NUI Galway, 1980).

O'Mordha, E., *Breifne: An early history of the Ua Ruairc Dynasty* (University College Dublin, 1998).

Kelly, J., *An outward looking community? Ribbonism and population mobilisation in Co. Leitrim 1836-1846* (PhD Thesis, University of Limerick 2005).

Traynor, Fr, *Papers,* Dromahair Library.